The L...

God's Purpose in the Season of Waiting

Steve Hawkins

Onwards and Upwards Publishers

Berkeley House, 11 Nightingale Crescent, Leatherhead,
Surrey, KT24 6PD.

www.onwardsandupwards.org

Printed in the UK by 4edge Limited.

ISBN: 978-1-910197-53-0
Typeface: Sabon LT
Graphic design: LM Graphic Design

About the Author

Steve Hawkins teaches English as a Second Language in London and is part of the New Zion Christian Fellowship family in Welwyn Garden City.

Having served the body of Christ for some time, he came to see that he was bound by degrees of legalism, through a visit to Toronto Airport Christian Fellowship. Here he was strongly impacted by the Father's love and now longs to see others enjoy genuine freedom in Jesus Christ.

Previously employed in both the catering and financial services industries, he now teaches students from all over the world in a large college.

The author of seven books, including 'From Legal to Regal' and 'Blood and Glory', he ministers today with a growing prophetic edge in leading worship, preaching and teaching.

The author can be contacted at:
steve.hawkins@cheerful.com

Steve longs to see those in the Body of Christ live in the freedom that Jesus has bought on the cross. If you would like him to speak or minister at an event, please contact him.

Dedicated to my wonderful pastors,
Peter and Rose Eldredge.

You show me the Father's Heart
and have modelled Christ's
abundant life so beautifully.

Contents

"Only in the darkness can you see
the stars."

– Martin Luther King Jr.

Foreword by Rose Eldridge

I have known Steve Hawkins for many years both as a friend and as his pastor.

Steve has authored several books and has an accurate prophetic ministry. He frequently preaches and teaches at church and has a gift of leading us all into Father's presence with his worship anointing. Steve has written and taught many new worship songs that are direct from his own unique walk with God.

'The Fourth Day' is written with great skill and knowledge of God's Word and takes you on a journey through many lives, bringing understanding and revelatory insight about issues that are seldom discussed. A very imaginative read.

Rose Eldridge
Pastor, New Zion Christian Fellowship
Welwyn Garden City

The Fourth Day

Introduction

Only God could possibly fathom the countless intricacies of how He works in our lives, whether we happen to see ourselves as currently prospering or finding life somewhat a trial.

Psalm 139:13-14
For You formed my inward parts;
You wove me in my mother's womb.
I will give thanks to You, for I am fearfully and wonderfully made;
Wonderful are Your works,
And my soul knows it very well.

Here it is in The Message (MSG):

Oh yes, you shaped me first inside, then out;
you formed me in my mother's womb.
I thank you, High God – you're breathtaking!
Body and soul, I am marvellously made!

We, finite beings, do our best; we think, we reason, we may pummel our brains and we may seek advice. We might even pray. As a dog with a bone, we hold on stubbornly to an apparent right to get a grasp on what God might be doing within our circumstances.

But there is a better way for us in whom the Holy Spirit has made His home; finite we might be, but mighty we are in Jesus Christ, in-filled by the supreme spirit of revelation – God the Holy Spirit Himself.

My prayer is that by the time you have finished this book, you will have yielded to the Rest of God – that 'God Rest' which is our inheritance. We have been designed to live from this place of rest, which lies within His Peace, the peace which is superior to, and supersedes, our reasoning (Proverbs 3:5).

He – God, that is – really likes being God. He is absolutely confident in who He is and has an excellent self-image! Being the very essence of Life itself, He is Joy personified; He has no rivals to His position and appears to be very competent indeed at His role of being the One True God. He has an unsurpassed record in individual, family, national and international management. He has never been wrong or had so much as an unrighteous thought, and has never lost an argument, let alone a fight. And He knows how to stand with the weak and frail. Our God doesn't only break down walls, He routinely walks *through* them.

I want to walk with you through some of those uncomfortable places in or on the borders of Panic Land, where we tend to wander and drift, sometimes even frantically searching – as a crestfallen golfer looks haplessly for his missing ball – for keys to relieving our discomfort when we have run out of answers or palpable solutions to a crisis.

Sometimes the waiting for a shift in a situation or, more specifically, for what we perceive to be the Lord's input into one, seems interminable. Ask Martha and Mary, whose beloved Lazarus had been dead three days. Jesus had not come, and their exhausted senses could not fathom His continued absence.

Of course, there's a key issue just there: our perceptions are not always quite on the ball, I think you'll admit.

We will also have a think about time. We are so conscious of it, of its fleeting nature on the one hand and its ability to drag us second by crawling second on the other. We are going to see that God sees it very differently and that we can too.

And we will see that there are occasions when we can exercise change from our position of authority in Christ Jesus.

So pull up a chair. Or a beanbag. As I write, we are in the latter throws of summer. I am a teacher and have recently returned to work, which generally means that some excellent weather is on the way; I'm going to have to enjoy most of it through the windows of a hot classroom. So whether you are indoors or out, sitting or horizontal, the Holy Spirit has snuck up alongside you to breathe His revelation into your heart.

Holy Spirit, we love you.

Come, please, right now and right here. Touch my inside eyes to see You and my inner ears to hear what you're saying.

Thank you. Amen.

To those of you who know Jesus Christ, the Holy Spirit is already inside you, of course, but it can't hurt to let Him know again that you're eager for His company! We have so underestimated His desire for our friendship.

You'll meet a bunch of prayers like the one above as you proceed through 'The Fourth Day'. Please join me in them; let's do this together in the company of the Holy Spirit, the Lord of Life.

The Fourth Day

CHAPTER ONE

The Fourth Day – Part I

"'He knows the way He taketh,' even if for the moment we do not."

J I Packer

He had died. And the family, friends and neighbours were distraught.

We know from the Bible that Lazarus had been sick, although the details of his maladies and deterioration are sketchy; probably, because they don't really matter in the grander scheme of things. The account that we have of Lazarus' passing is, nevertheless, very accessible to the majority of us as we walk along the avenue of his loved ones' grief. We recognise, perhaps, where we have 'been there'.

Where is 'there'? It is not only the potent mix of frazzled emotions that are faced when we lose a loved one; it is also the place where, despite our straining to 'know', we cannot fathom answers.

And yet, when the previously absent miracle-worker finally arrived in Bethany, He cried. *Jesus cried tears.* The Son of God wept with this family. Sometimes we forget that the all-glorious Messiah had left behind His majesty in Heaven and walked as a man. Not that majesty equates to emotional distance. But the Son of God – He was and is truly God – was also the Son of Man. He had come to earth as a complete man, as one filled with the vibrant power and presence of the Holy Spirit. And Jesus had specifically said that He would only do what He saw His Father doing (John 5 and John 12) – here was to be our blueprint for life, if you like. As complicated as we tend to make life at times, Jesus set out an example of simplicity, one which left no space for dead ends or possible burnout; that we should only involve ourselves in what we see the Father doing through the witness of the Holy Spirit. We are going to look at this in more depth later.

We read of the family's plight and sense their desperation and the dread that comes from 'not knowing'. As we face our own trials we would like some kind of explanation. I mean, *at the actual time of the crisis* – that's when we would like to have it. The much championed benefit of hindsight is all very well, Lord, but we want to appeal to You: our brains are befuddled as to what is happening when the crisis is at its peak. We are looking to drop anchor but can't remember where it is.

However, as we read in Scripture, the Holy Spirit can reveal to us many aspects of God's character that we have not as yet known.

Despite appearances, our Father really has left nothing to chance.

Our Need

It is so very important for us to understand that we are in great, continual need of our Teacher, the Holy Spirit. He is precious and we were designed to relate with Him; we need His presence and insights so very much. Just one word from Him and everything can change. If He appears to be saying nothing, something significant is still going on, something deep, and something required and crucial concerning us. As He leads us into a greater depth of maturity, His silences can be as significant as when He speaks.

> "God will never disappoint us. He loves us and has only one
> purpose for us: holiness, which in His Kingdom equals joy."
> *Elizabeth Elliot*

God is always, regardless of our perceptions, leading us into greater light and into a more intimate knowledge of Himself. And this is exactly what He was about, leading up to the fourth day following Lazarus demise.

I encourage you to stop for a minute and refresh your memory of the account of Lazarus found in John 11:1-46. The story can be found in the Appendix of this book, on page 119.

I wonder how many of the emotions revealed you and I can relate to: the sense of despondency and desolation, a chink of light igniting optimism, an assumption (perhaps better described as an inner demand?) as to what Jesus is going to do, crushing disappointment and a feeling of abandonment and loneliness; and later, mind numbing amazement, wonder, joy and celebration. But we have not quite arrived at that later place of release just yet, if you will bear with me. We are still at that place described by Michel Quoist:

> "Everything seems grey and sombre as when a fog blots out the sun and enshrouds the earth. Everything is an effort, everything is difficult and I am heavy footed and slow ... in the middle of the desert, suddenly you have disappeared. I call, and you do not answer."

Here's the thing. Martha and Mary could not have done any more than they had done, could they? They had loved Lazarus and they loved Jesus. They trusted the Lord as frail humans can; they knew He was capable of exercising the miraculous. They had believed that Jesus could and would turn this miserable situation around. He only had to come and heal. If He cared, that is what He would do and that was the bottom line.

Except it wasn't. He had not come.

CHAPTER TWO

The Fourth Day – Part II

"Jesus said to them, 'Do you believe that I am able to do this?'"

Matthew 9:28

Many of us have learned, and continue to learn, that our 'bottom lines' are often nowhere near the actual base of where God is taking us. The very fact that we squirm and writhe in our restlessness is in itself evidence that we have not yet learned to truly trust. We are to some degree still seeking to walk by our natural sight rather than by faith.

In a later chapter we are going to examine one key lesson that I have learned about faith, and that (as Jesus quoted to the infernal accuser in a bleak, desert place) men and women really do fully live by the words of His mouth rather than by bread for the stomach.

In verse 6 of John 11 we see that Jesus makes a clear calculation. Having iterated Jesus' love for Martha, Mary and Lazarus, the Bible tells us that He purposely made a decision: to stay where He was for two more days.

Jesus' assessments are never mistakes. He calculates from the very source of absolute wisdom that He is. To say He *has* wisdom is to understate the truth; He *is* wisdom.

We so struggle at times with our self-dependencies. God is in the business of radically changing us through many of the paths we walk:

> "...God wants to change us, and we don't want to be changed. Not really, not the kind of change God wants. I mean really change. Not cosmetic surgery but radical surgery – that's what God is after. He intends to reach down into the guts of our soul..."
>
> *Ron Dunn*

Can we see here that Jesus did actually answer the crisis He was presented with? His decision was based upon the true, not perceived, reality of the situation in hand, His love for the people we have mentioned, and a premise that undergirded everything that He ever did. He described it like this in John 5 after healing a lame man who had been ill for some thirty-eight years. It is almost an impossible question to pose but it does goes through your mind: why did this man have to wait thirty-eight years? As with many such quandaries, one can only really return to the moments when Jesus *did* meet the man's need and praise Him for His compassion, love and power.

John 5:17
But He answered them, "My Father is working until now, and I Myself am working."

John 5:19
Therefore Jesus answered and was saying to them, "Truly, truly, I say to you, the Son can do nothing of Himself, unless it is something He sees the Father doing; for whatever the Father does, these things the Son also does in like manner."

The English Revised Version puts this verse in this way:

But Jesus answered, "I assure you that the Son can do nothing alone. He does only what he sees his Father doing. The Son does the same things that the Father does."

So there is the Bible's answer. Jesus healed the man when He did, because that is when He saw the Father acting on his behalf.

Back home in Judea, Mary and Martha were concluding, in their anguish, grief and absence of heavenly perspective, that Jesus had failed to act. I mean, *where was He?* How many of us, likewise, have assumed that no tangible intervention or word from Jesus has meant that He was off duty?

Or, the accuser may beat our brain with the notion that we are probably just too sinful, or not spiritual enough, to matter to Jesus. The enemy might even tell you that God is speaking to you but you're just incapable of hearing Him. Tortuous condemnation piles upon condemnation.

On the contrary, with all His heart and in complete conviction, Jesus chose to stay away for an exactly measured period of time. It was His choice. No one in Judea had failed Him.

> *Lord Jesus – we admit our need of Your revelation! We have so much to learn – so much unreality to un-learn! We have to acknowledge that Your ways are perfect because you always act in perfect love.*

Verse 15 is sensational, might I suggest? Jesus expresses His joy that His tarrying away from Judea is going to bear fruit – that His disciples "may believe". Their faith walk is clearly of huge importance to the Saviour.

You see, there is 'believing' and there is 'BELIEVING'. Many acknowledge and declare belief in Jesus which, when tested, amounts to a kind of formula: "I'll go along with Him and trust Him as long as I can track what He's doing." It's believing in Him on our own terms, which require Him to act as we would act, in other words, *in our image.*

Really this is a shallow apology for genuine trust and, I imagine, most of us have to grow from there. This kind of believing creates a Jesus of our own making, a Jesus in our own image and expectations. He does not condemn us for that – He understands how we function – but if we are going to grow up in our faith walk and grow in 'real' relationship with the 'real' Jesus Christ, let me gently assure you that He is going to undo many of our false assumptions about Him. When you love someone to the extent that He loves us, you want him or her to know you in true intimacy – in truth – in reality. The Holy Spirit is exceptionally good at this kind of tailored work in our lives. And... He is absolutely confident in His ability to do it 'just right' for each of us.

That's what Jesus is saying in verse 15. "You think you know Me – you profess belief – but I am glad because you are about to discover something much more wonderful!"

Jesus arrives in Bethany. Lazarus has been dead now for four days. Jesus is not about to receive a warm greeting so much as mystified enquiries.

Four Days

Four days. A calculated period of time. Perhaps the following commentary from *www.biblegateway.com* will provide some useful perspective concerning the belief systems of the day:

> "The scene now shifts to Bethany, near Jerusalem, as Jesus arrives and finds that Lazarus has been in the tomb for four days. Burials normally took place on the day of the death (cf. Acts 5:6-10), so he has been dead for four days. For Jews this probably signifies that Lazarus is clearly dead and beginning to decay (cf. m. Yebamot 16:3). A later Jewish text that cites an authority from the early third century A.D. says the mourners should continue to come to the tomb for three days because the dead person continues to be present there. Mourning is at its height on the third day, presumably because it is the last time the dead person will be present there. 'Bar Kappara taught: Until three days [after death] the soul keeps on returning to the grave, thinking that it will go back [into the body]; but when it sees that the facial features have become disfigured, it departs and abandons it [the body]' (Genesis Rabbah 100:7; cf. Leviticus Rabbah 18:1; Ecclesiastes Rabbah 12:6). Thus, the reference to the fourth day may be quite significant for setting the scene for another dramatic miracle."

Jesus deliberately waits until all natural hope has gone. He waits until no one else can help. He waits until the situation is hopeless, until it is final. It's a painful lesson, but as we look back now at the event, and as countless millions have learned something critically important about the nature of our Lord and Saviour, I have to say that I am glad that these events happened as they did. If that sounds heartless or dispassionate towards the individuals, families and the community involved, then let us remind ourselves that Jesus, too, said that He was glad that He had not been in Bethany when Lazarus was ill. He knew that something far greater was going to be demonstrated than that which everyone was clamouring for.

I mean, life is like that, isn't it? Wouldn't you agree that there are times when we are able to appreciate what we have learned, and even come to see aspects of who we have grown to become, through an uncomfortable trial? How we would have avoided it if we could have!

Revelation

The Holy Spirit is about His business, and His business is the Father's business. He knows that we are frail and yet we are in dire need of knowing God in reality.

> John 17:3 (NIV)
> *Now this is eternal life: that they know you, the only true God, and Jesus Christ, whom you have sent.*

This verse reads very powerfully in the Amplified Bible:

> *And this is eternal life: [it means] to know (to perceive, recognise, become acquainted with, and understand) You, the only true and real God, and [likewise] to know Him, Jesus [as the] Christ (the Anointed One, the Messiah), Whom You have sent.*

This process of becoming acquainted involves a great deal of 'unknowing'. We have to un-learn much of what we have come to believe about God, about ourselves and about the lives we lead.

Have you ever felt wary about meeting someone for the first time of whom you had previously heard others' negative opinions? Then you meet them; you decide that you are going to make up your own mind and find yourself pleasantly surprised with your new acquaintance.

Remember that we are all described in the Bible as sheep. Well, sheep need to be led. We may think we learn a lot through life but I have discovered something:

Sheep are sheep.

I am, and will always be, sheep-like. I do not want conflict, thank you very much; but much of our faith walk is about the clash between Kingdom Reality and our own earthbound mindsets. Having the mind of Christ in Kingdom Life is an inestimable asset, nevertheless we will never get even close to fully grasping God's nature this side of eternity. He will continue to surprise us, and He will continue to move in our lives in such a way that we have to live by faith. We sheep need our Shepherd. We do not mature into self-dependency. We mature *out* of it. Speaking of our human efforts to work things out, Joyce Meyer writes:

"God has no choice but to back off and wait until we have finished trying to handle things ourselves."

Before they were seduced by lies, Adam and Eve lived lives of majestic maturity. They simply aligned themselves with God's purposes and provision, and they wanted for nothing.

As we look at this account of Lazarus together, I am not going to suggest that every disaster that Jesus walks into is transformed into an idyllic ending. That is not the point. The point is that we tend to approach difficult situations with our desired solutions and outcomes already entrenched in our expectations. Rather, our desire needs to be that God orchestrates the outcome. And that outcome will, in most cases, probably be other than you and I have imagined, and may or may not involve our input.

"Lord, You could have... You should have... Why didn't You...?"

Let's all sign our names to these questions; we have probably thought and prayed them on many occasions. But we can be misguided. Our complaints and protests, though entirely understandable, are actually misinformed because we are dealing with God, our magnificent, all-good God. Let me guarantee you that there are elements in play that are invisible to us as God takes the reins of our darkest hours.

This situation in Bethany was a closed case to the locals. Jesus should have been there and He wasn't, and now it was too late. Even the three days of grace period had expired and all that remained of Lazarus was a rotting, putrefying corpse and painful confusion.

It's interesting, however, that upon leaving for Bethany, Jesus had described Lazarus as "him". In Jesus' mind, Lazarus was a long, long way from final departure because He already knew from His Father what He was going to do.

Reversal

No one could have imagined the reversal of this predicament. As Jesus calls Lazarus from the tomb, the human race learns an unequalled, unparalleled lesson: this Jesus Christ can even reverse death. The Scriptures that teach of resurrection are embodied in this man, Jesus Christ. He doesn't just *deal with* resurrection; He isn't *about* it; He *is* the resurrection, the eternal source of vibrant power, the essence of unstoppable life. This is the same Jesus who, in Genesis, spoke into the empty void and from His mere words nothing became something. Everything has come from Him. Our Jesus is so magnificently Lord, and He reigns over all creation, seen and unseen.

I imagine that I have many untrodden roads yet to tread in this walk of the miraculous, but I can tell you that I have learned incrementally through 'lost' situations in my life that the Redeemer is well able to reach them, transforming and even bringing reversals in issues that concern me. Later you will read about some of them.

Jesus encourages Martha to look beyond head belief and to grasp Him as He is really is. "Martha you are disappointed but I am the resurrection." He is saying, "I am in your now, and now is what matters."

Jesus encourages us to reach for Him and to hold on to Him. The time to press into Him and His miracle touch is always *now*, even when our minds and emotions are past knowing. Now is always the time to make new discoveries about our Lord and Saviour.

CHAPTER THREE

Joseph

"Admittedly, God doesn't always deliver us from our problems in the way we want Him to."

Robert J Morgan

When I take up residence in my heavenly mansion, I hope to be in the same street as Joseph. *The* Joseph. Jacob's Joseph. I don't doubt that Mary's Joseph has a raft of precious insights to share (an understatement!) but I have always felt that Joseph of technicolour garment fame has been, and will continue to be, a significant biblical character in my own faith walk. I know I'm not the only one, as knowing nods have greeted me when I have spoken of him with congregations.

He is an example of how to respond when everything appears to go shockingly wrong. Especially when you are sure you have had a promise or two concerning a situation, suggesting that the complete opposite should have happened. It can come as quite a shock. R T Kendall writes:

"The first thing we notice about Joseph's preparation is that it began without any advance notice."

One night, during a stormy season in my life, I had a dream. In this dream I saw myself running down a hill through some thick forest. 'Thick forest' just about summed up where I was at in my life. I was besieged by confusion and anxiety at that time with no real idea of a way of escape. As I glimpsed myself in the dream moving through the mass of trees, I saw a man running down the hill, parallel to me alongside the edge of the forest. I knew that this was Jesus. God was showing me that although I felt clueless in my situation, He was nearby, He was at hand. Sometimes it really is enough to know only that. He promised, and continues to promise, that He will never leave us. Indeed, those of us who are born of the Spirit have His Spirit residing within our own spirits.

It is also easy, I find, to gloss over some of the gritty details of an account such as Joseph's when you've read it several times and it has become familiar. Somehow, with future readings, already knowing the happy ending soothes away some of our discomfort as we read of the process of God's work in his life. That's the luxury that we have as a reader. Joseph's experience was every bit as challenging and gut-wrenching as the account in the Bible describes.

Have you noticed how most testimonies that are shared in our churches glorify the Lord for what He has already done? Amen to that, rightly so! It occurs to me that less testimonies are shared when people are in the middle of their process. Perhaps that is actually the time when the Body of Christ can stand alongside the person. It is a powerful time to testify because God is moving and delivering and strengthening the person at that time.

I love the prophetic. I have always known, pretty much since I was saved, that the prophetic was going to be an area of ministry appointed for me. I am sure you appreciate, though, that there is a cost to moving in it. I believe that the Holy Spirit would have a far greater proportion of the Body of Christ operating in the prophetic with words of knowledge, dreams, significant 'now' words (which we know as 'rhema' words), pictures and impressions laid upon our hearts. The office of a prophet is something rather different, but I believe that God would have the vast majority of us speaking in tongues and prophesying. We are to be a proclaiming, decreeing people!

What we absolutely do all have is a destiny in Jesus: He has plans for us; He knows us by name; we are each entirely unique; and we have a personal space in Jesus' heart and in His Kingdom ministry.

Destiny, not Assembly Line

You were individually crafted, according to Psalm 139. You did not fall off a cosmic assembly line. You are not here by accident, regardless of the circumstances of your birth and family (non-family?) background.

You do not just happen to be here because of evolution. The theory of evolution can cause, in my opinion, a crack in many people's life foundations. God wants to, and can, heal this. He wants to show you that He designed you personally and set you free from the undermining nonsense that tries to dictate that you are here without His prior knowledge, fashioning and purpose.

> *Lord Jesus, thank you for the power of Your Word. You say that You formed us in our mother's womb, that You saw us in the hidden place and, equally, have seen all of our days. We reject the notion that we are anything other than desired, unique individuals. We denounce the lie of evolution and release ourselves to discover increasingly your love for us and holy purpose for our lives. In Jesus' name. Amen!*

I hardly need say, I hope, that this applies to all of us – black and white, young and old, and from every background, nation and tongue. Amen! R T Kendall says:

> "God has more in mind for you that even your wildest fancy can grasp. God has a plan for your life."

Joseph, likewise, had a destiny for his life, and although we may not be called to be the Prime Minister of our nation, we will, to some degree, be called to a level of leadership.

I love it that our pastors at home regularly remind us, "You are all leaders." I love it that at any moment you may be asked to minister in some way: to pray, to share, to bless someone, to make the tea or maybe sweep the lobby.

Back to Joseph in a moment, but I want to tell you about my first morning at my precious church, New Zion Christian Fellowship in Welwyn Garden City in the UK.

I was a little nervous but excited. I had only known for two to three weeks that the Lord was moving me there. He had spoken to me about that in a local pub after I had preached at New Zion (as a visiting speaker). It was one of those 'faith' moments where the Holy Spirit touched my spirit as someone dropped a casual line in the conversation and instantly I knew that this was my new church. That faith moment from Him cleared the way and I had no doubts.

As I walked into the church on that 'first' day in my new spiritual home, where pre-meeting prayer was taking place, I felt out of my depth. First time nerves, maybe. We had a visiting minister that day, a gentleman of significant standing and ministry in the Elim movement in the UK. I can't have been in the building for more than five minutes, when Rose (Peter and Rose are our pastors) handed me the microphone, asking me to pray for the minister. As soon as she did so, I began to prophesy, and it was as if I was raised to the level of spirit life of the church; by that I mean, I was being incorporated in the Spirit, I was being planted into this family of the Body of Christ, and my sense of self-doubt was dissolved.

Profile

Joseph did what a lot of us do. (Well, you may disagree.) Having had revelations from God, I put it to you that he shared too early. I think that we sometimes do that. God speaks to us and we share it, maybe quite openly, thereby inviting all and sundry to speak back into our life, perhaps before the Holy Spirit has Himself begun to clothe and confirm that word, nurturing it in our heart. Some people will pep you up and others will cast doubts on what God has said to you. I am not trying to make rules here – far from it – but I think we need to be wise about whom we share our revelation with, and when.

Joseph told his whole family. As a result, they flipped. So began the testing of God's word in Joseph. It's hard when your nearest and dearest are unable to see what you have seen, or cast you off as a dreamer.

If God has told you that you are going to be a leader of significant status in the Kingdom, I would respectfully advise you to major on continuing to love those around you rather than advertising your 'good' news! God knows how to promote you, if that is what He is going to do. It may not involve an earthly promotion at all. You may remain almost completely unknown. Are you ready for that? But if a public profile is on God's heart for you, you are going to need some preparation if you are going to stand firm and flourish, and that's what became Joseph's master class.

Pressure and Denial

John 12:24
Truly, truly, I say to you, unless a grain of wheat falls into the earth and dies, it remains alone; but if it dies, it bears much fruit.

This speaks of Jesus' death, resurrection and the subsequent explosion of Church growth, but it also points to the principal of apparent reversal. We see it across the Bible. We may not all become kings and queens, such as Esther and David, but we do have a Kingdom destiny and we need to stand for it. The enemy will oppose it. He is jealous of us. He forfeited his destiny and place in heaven and doesn't want us to be effective as we live for the Kingdom of God. Every step of progress we make in the Kingdom displaces enemy influence both in our own lives and in our spheres of influence.

Perhaps, as happened with me, the enemy tried to sow some weeds early in your life.

Bullying

I was horribly bullied at school. It went on for years.

Nobody seemed to be able to help – and I mean *nobody*, not even the authorities that would have had a mandate to do so. Today, in 2014, such treatment exacted upon an individual would be classed as abuse. I am not going to go into the details of my battle at school – and I hasten to add that it was an excellent school in most respects – as it will not serve our purpose. The point is that I had a prophetic call on my life which God has said would impact the nations. Satan knew this and tried to sow as much fear, intimidation and control into my early school years as possible. You can see that this was a counter assignment.

Prophetic people are often spontaneous types. I wouldn't wish to put anyone in a box, but a lot of us who operate in the prophetic seem to tick that way. We want to be open to the Holy Spirit's flow and go with it. We can be uncomfortable with a lot of planning and formula.

Our lives in Jesus are destined for immeasurable blessing, and counter assignments are common.

> "You are under the new covenant of unmerited favour through Jesus' finished work."
>
> *Joseph Prince*

Joseph had counter assignments too, but let us be encouraged that God, always a step ahead, was mixing such incidents and circumstances into His golden purpose for him.

You can read the account of all that happened to Joseph in and from Genesis 37. Four chapters later, Joseph has been elevated to second-in-command over all Egypt, second only to Pharaoh who was considered to be a god. That's a sensational advancement! Along the way, we read that Joseph was despised by his family, thrown into a pit under the threat of death, sold to strangers, bought by a stranger and taken to his house to work for him, accused of rape, and thrown into a prison where he suffered the agony of crushing disappointment – that's a word that we are going to unpack – as he appeared to have been forgotten by those who could have spoken on his behalf. Joseph would have made an excellent speaker on abandonment issues!

All this must have seemed a far cry from the excitement he had known following his dreams.

He also had a prominent married woman offer herself time and again into his hands, which he kept to himself. Here was an honest, godly man who honoured God. In honouring Him, he resisted her advances and the temptation she served him. I like what Madame Jeanne Guyon says about resisting temptations:

> "Be very careful in your attitude towards them. If you attempt to struggle directly with these temptations, you will only strengthen them; and in the process of this struggle, your soul will be drawn away from its intimate relationship with the Lord."

In other words, Joseph was able to determine to turn his face from those temptations because he was already in that place of intimacy with his God.

All through this catalogue of trial, the Bible says that God was with him. Dare we underestimate the power of those words? Do you know that God is not only with you but inside you? Sometimes in life's circumstances we can feel very lost, but the truth is that we are so very found.

> *Lord, we pause for a moment. We take a moment just to be. We are here with You. We are in You, and You are in us. Thank you for abiding in us so strongly and faithfully. We may not understand You or our circumstances at times, but please continue to express your Kingdom in and through our lives. Your work in our hearts is worth it, dear Lord. You are ours, and we are yours. In Jesus' name. Amen.*

At the conclusion of this process of fiery trial, a gifted, called but impetuous young man has been refined into a mature leader. Take a look at the fruit at this stage of his life. Jesus said that we define the health of a tree's roots by the quality of its fruit (Matthew 7:16).

Before I remind you of Joseph's gracious response to his brothers when his opportunity to rain down retribution upon them arrives, I have a confession to share about my – at times – sorry attitude when I am driving.

What happens when I am in the car? What metamorphosis of heart takes place once I am strapped into my nippy little Citroen C3? I have a red C3. Officially, according to the brochure, it is 'wicked red'. But I can't blame the vehicle. It's the same transformation that took place when I was strapped into my (previous) Ford Focus and in my Ford Escort before that!

As a work in progress, I seem to offer a lot less grace than I receive, at times. I seem to see this unwelcome aspect of my character when I am on the road. But I am learning not to berate myself or to indulge in mental self-flagellation. Rather, I celebrate His grace and His righteousness in me. It is truly the kindness of the Lord that causes us to change, and He will finish what He has started.

The Crucible

The Crucible Theatre in Sheffield, UK is a small venue that seats just short of one thousand spectators. The theatre is so designed that audience members (for theatrical productions) and spectators (for sports events – notably a prestigious annual snooker tournament) sit in an intimate atmosphere. Indeed, no watching individual sits further than twenty metres from the action.

Crucibles are about being closed in. A useful comment can be found from Wikipedia:

> "A crucible is a container that can withstand very high temperatures ... While crucibles historically were usually made from clay, they can be made from any material that withstands temperatures high enough to melt or otherwise alter its contents."

Joseph had to grow up and become a man with broad shoulders and a generous heart. Time in the fire of God does that. God's crucible can be an unpleasant yet precious place to find oneself. It can be one of those costly places where His peace and a set of coarse circumstances meet. Our outer husk is melted, and God's hand touches and brings transformation to the heart.

Remember Joseph's dream as he saw his brothers and parents bowing before him. He is about to witness its fulfilment. But see how Joseph responds:

Genesis 42:26-31
When Joseph came home, they brought into the house to him the present which was in their hand and bowed to the ground before him. Then he asked them about their welfare, and said, "Is your old father well, of whom you spoke? Is he still alive?" They said, "Your servant our father is well; he is still alive." They bowed down in homage. As he lifted his eyes and saw his brother Benjamin, his mother's son, he said, "Is this your youngest brother, of whom you spoke to me?" And he said, "May God be gracious to you, my son." Joseph hurried out for he was deeply stirred over his brother, and he sought a place to weep; and he entered his chamber and wept there. Then he washed his face and came out; and he controlled himself and said, "Serve the meal."

The Voice puts verses 30 and 31 thus:

Joseph hurried from the room because he was overwhelmed with affection for his brother and was afraid he would cry in front of everyone. So he went into a private room and wept there. After he regained his composure, he washed his face and came out. With a controlled voice, he commanded his servants.

This is a man who has been through the dealings of God. Joseph exhibits compassion and a soft heart towards his brothers who have so wronged him. He exhibits the character of God. His brothers, terrified at the prospect of their little brother (now exalted ruler) getting even with them, cower before him – but revenge is not on his radar. He responds with love, the prime evidence of the fruit of the Spirit. This is a man who has understood his life's path from a sanctified perspective.

So many of those who surround us in our streets, workplaces and hives of leisure are convinced that God is looking to get even with them. But as R T Kendall comments:

"That is the way many people react. They think God is out to get them ... Do you really think God will be satisfied if He punishes you? What satisfied God's justice? One thing: the death of His Son."

As we read on in Genesis we see how Joseph is reunited with his father and welcomes the family to Egypt, more than seventy of them! God has done all things well.

And He is doing all things well in your and my life, too, be it in calm waters or in the storm. God had His way with Joseph and saved a nation.

Some of our crises may be about more than just us.

CHAPTER FOUR

The Need to Know

"Some of us pray demands. Some of us pray complaints. Some of us pray knowing, and some of us pray not knowing. But prayer is the attitude that you hold in your heart."[1]

Iyania Vanzant

In the 1980s' British BBC television sitcom, 'Yes, Prime Minister', the hapless leader of the nation struggles with the machinations of government office and his apparently unsupportive, conspiring ministers! James Hacker is the Prime Minister in this popular comedy, and Bernard Woolley is a savvy member of the civil service team. Here is an excerpt from the script:

James Hacker:	Are you telling me the Foreign Office is keeping something from me?
Bernard Woolley:	Yes.
James Hacker:	Well, what?

---

[1] Read more at www.brainyquote.com/quotes/keywords/not_knowing_2.html# KA6R7HjRmv9xU4ku.99

Bernard Woolley:	I don't know; they're keeping it from me too.
James Hacker:	How do you know?
Bernard Woolley:	I don't know.
James Hacker:	You just said that the Foreign Office was keeping something from me. How do you know if you don't know?
Bernard Woolley:	I don't know specifically what, Prime Minister, but I do know the Foreign Office always keep everything from everybody. It's normal practice.

We think we need to know.

But we don't.

It's a habit that we have acquired over the years; it's entrenched so deeply that we would say that we are wired that way. That's how it feels. But the feeling is not telling us the truth.

The feeling is based on the fact that we have sought to control our circumstances for so long. There may be many understandable reasons for that, and I don't underestimate the challenges or abuses that may have provoked and buffeted us. But to live in the Spirit, change needs to come, and it is coming because it has to.

Young children don't, I would suggest, behave in the same way. They haven't learned to yet. Sometimes when I ask young children about their plans for a particular day, they answer, "I don't know." It doesn't matter to them either that they don't. They are walking out their young days in trust, knowing that those who are looking after them have taken care of the details. Not that they don't ask a lot of questions, but they seem to be satisfied that as long as someone in charge knows then that is all that is required.

Adam and Eve didn't need to know. They lived in perfect peace, in perfect communion and friendship with God who would meet them in the Garden. It was only when the snake lied to them and told them that they "needed to know" that disorder came into the picture.

Satan propositioned Eve with an apparently fascinating piece of fruit.

Genesis 3:4-5
The serpent said to the woman, "You surely will not die! For God knows that in the day you eat from it your eyes will be opened, and you will be like God, knowing good and evil."

You see, Adam and Eve were already alive, fully alive! God Himself had breathed into them. They were to live like that – breathing His breath and living in transparent abandon to their Father and provider. All that they needed to learn and know was provided and shared with them. If that sounds like dependence, then yes, it was. God's heart was to be a friend and Father to them. But Satan said, "That's not enough. See how you lack. See what more you could have."

It was a lie. Satan could not give them more. He could only give them something different and that would be something they had not been designed to carry: an independent spirit.

Think about it for a moment. We don't really need to know on many of those occasions when we are longing to, do we? In a crisis, we think we need to know, but really we just need to know that someone who is able to help us knows!

If a loved one suffers a serious accident, you don't have to know the particular details of what needs to happen in the operating theatre. You are satisfied to know that the clinical staff have the situation covered. You want someone to say, "Leave it with me. I know what I'm doing."

Well, that is perhaps true to a point. We tend to remember when someone has given us such assurances and then let us down through incompetence or negligence; this then fuels our desire to know details just in case there is anything we can do or say to guarantee a positive outcome. When talking with individuals, we may summarise what has been said as a kind of security net. Fix, fix, fix! Tweak, tweak! Meddle, meddle! We are trying to exercise control and gain a foothold in the midst of our insecurity.

"You people are telling me what you think I want to know.
I want to know what is actually happening."

Creighton Abrams

This weakness that we inherited through the Fall sends us on mental and emotional roller-coasters. Our imagination – that God given realm designed to picture opportunities and dreams of faith – becomes a muddled, disordered playground for fear and negative suggestion to destabilise us out of our peace and rest. We know that Jesus said that He is our peace and that this peace is 'otherworldly'. It's in the spirit realm, not the realm of reason.

God had been no killjoy in barring Adam and Eve from that one tree in the Garden. It was a glorious, unspoiled garden blooming with bud and fruit. If we, on earth, are able to plant a lavish garden, can you imagine what this one must have looked like and contained? God was fathering the couple with His warning about the one tree, but they succumbed to reasoning rather than staying in the place of peace and supply that was their life and inheritance.

In Eden, nothing was judged to be good and nothing was judged to be evil. There was no reasoning of this nature. Everything was simply of God and of His doing and completeness; there was no measuring of how good anything was because it was immeasurably of God! It was God-standard, which meant supreme excellence beyond words or human judgement!

By eating the fruit, Adam and Eve "had their eyes opened". Well, that's what Satan had promised them, but of course it was a lie. In essence, the opposite happened. Their 'faith eyes' were blinded, their vision of their best friend, God, and all He had made them to be and given them to prosper, fogged over. They would now have to resort to making judgements, estimations and reasoning, when previously life had been so gloriously simple.

We don't really 'need to know' a lot of the time. Not at all. We need to simply yield that insecurity and hankering for control to our Father and trust Him.

We see this popular scripture in our Bibles – on tea towels, mugs and a host of varied Christian merchandise:

Proverbs 3:5-6
*Trust in the Lord with all your heart
And do not lean on your own understanding.*

In all your ways acknowledge Him,
And He will make your paths straight.

Here it is in The Message (MSG):

Trust God from the bottom of your heart;
don't try to figure out everything on your own.
Listen for God's voice in everything you do, everywhere you go;
he's the one who will keep you on track.

Jesus spoke of our sustenance being sourced from the words from God's mouth; therefore, we need to calm our flesh down, reckon it dead – it was crucified, right? – and realise once again that we were designed to walk out our lives in peace and in divine order, relying on what we know we have heard from the Lord. Revelation from the Holy Spirit never contains confusion.

God knows how to reach you; He knows how to enable you to hear Him. It would help if we would de-clutter ourselves from our own mental and emotional thrashing about, as a desperate non-swimmer unwittingly hinders their rescuer. The fight is in our minds and God says to us:

Isaiah 26:3
The steadfast of mind You will keep in perfect peace,
Because he trusts in You.

That can take a fair bit of discipline on our part. When the mental theatrics and somersaults assail us, we can speak to our minds and command them to become subservient to our spirit man: "Mind – I'm talking to you. Settle down. I have the mind of Christ. Peace is my portion. God is well able to speak to me in His peace." We have the authority to keep ourselves under His authority!

In this way, we will eat not from chaos, not from the Tree of the Knowledge of Good and Evil, but from the Tree of Life.

This tree has peaceable fruit, of Holy Spirit revelation. In Christ Jesus, this is the way to go, just as Jesus demonstrated it as He walked the earth, busying Himself only with what He saw the Father doing.

In the world, learning seems to be about being able to manage complications! In the Kingdom, it is about learning to keep ourselves in the rest of the Holy Spirit, walking in His revelation.

Let us draw this chapter to a close with a final word from 'Yes, Prime Minister'. In this excerpt, Sir Humphrey Appleby joins the scene, the Prime Minister's manipulative Personal Private Secretary. They are discussing who should shoulder the responsibility for a lapse of protocol.

James Hacker:	But it wasn't my fault. I didn't know he was being bugged.
Bernard Woolley:	Prime Minister, you are deemed to have known. You are ultimately responsible.
James Hacker:	Why wasn't I told?
Sir Humphrey Appleby:	The Home Secretary might not have felt the need to inform you.
James Hacker:	Why?
Sir Humphrey Appleby:	Perhaps he didn't know either. Or perhaps he'd been advised that you did not need to know.
James Hacker:	Well, I did need to know.
Bernard Woolley:	Apparently the fact that you needed to know was not known at the time that the now known need to know was known, and therefore those that needed to advise and inform the Home Secretary perhaps felt that the information that he needed as to whether to inform the highest authority of the known information was not yet known and therefore there was no authority for the authority to be informed because the need to know was not at this time known or needed.
James Hacker:	What!

CHAPTER FIVE

Unfair Accusation

"There is only one way of victory over the bitterness and rage that comes naturally to us – to will what God wills brings peace."

Amy Carmichael

I remember reading and being hugely impacted by international minister and writer John Bevere's testimony of God's dealings with him as he suffered at the hands of an unrighteous leader in his church. I say 'at the hands' of the leader although, in truth, it is more helpful for us to understand that no one ever takes us from God's hands. Others' hands merely become His tools in many situations. As we read in the first chapter from Elizabeth Elliott, God is about the business of developing genuine holiness in us.

John learned, as a young leader, the power of God's redeeming intervention as we allow Him to be our vindicator. Let me share some of this with you.

It was a vital lesson for him to learn, in light of the path that His Kingdom walk and career were going to take. Of course, he did not know the significance of this at the time of the conflict. But God knew. And God knew how to fashion a circumstance that would educate the young preacher in a key lesson of life. We would do well to listen up.

John was a youth pastor and part of a church leadership team. There was no doubt that God had a call on his life.

We all do. You do too. We tend to link the idea of a 'call' to be either a very visible ministry or a widely recognised one. It may well be one of those, or both, but it need not be. Most of God's heroes are only truly known to Him. I love hearing testimonies of servants of God whose endeavours have come to light after many, many years of faithful, unnoticed service and ministry. I say 'unnoticed' – you know what I mean, I'm sure. It only really matters that He notices what we do.

John ran into some trouble. Yes, that can happen in the church. Another member of the leadership team took offence because his son had confided with John some personal information concerning that leader's family's lifestyle. As a result, the boy's father made complaints against John to the senior pastor. John was distraught. Not only were the allegations made against him unfounded, but also John could not see how he was going to be believed alongside a senior, respected leader.

To add to the poisonous pot, this fellow briefed against the senior pastor too, telling John that the pastor was against him. It must have all been quite bewildering for the young Mr Bevere.

I am sure you know this Biblical premise concerning our conflicts in the earthly realm, but allow me to remind you:

Ephesians 6:12
For our struggle is not against flesh and blood, but against the rulers, against the powers, against the world forces of this darkness, against the spiritual forces of wickedness in the heavenly places.

The New Life Version says:

Our fight is not with people. It is against the leaders and the powers and the spirits of darkness in this world...

Oh my goodness! Don't we just want to fight our corner in situations like this! Everything inside us screams, "Justice! I want justice!" We pray (not unwisely) that the Holy Spirit will work in the situation to bring everything into the light and yet... deep down, we might be praying more urgently, if we are honest, that we will be vindicated.

"Lord save me. Help me. Defend me." These are good, heartfelt prayers.

We may go a step further. "Lord, bring down my enemy. Slash him, Lord! Trip him up! Humiliate him!"

Perhaps it depends on how angry we are.

I believe it is fine to be angry at injustices and to express them fully to God. Yes, *fully*. I remember, quite early in my faith walk, a visiting speaker coming to my church. While prophesying over me, he reassured me that God could handle my "pounding His chest with my fists" (these were his words, or similar) when I got frustrated. You may consider this irreverent, but I have come to see that we can be absolutely transparent with the One who is absolutely, transparently pure and good. He is not fazed by our outbursts although it's probably a good idea to still ourselves sooner than later so that we can listen more effectively!

John Bevere struggled with a sense of isolation. He firmly believed that he and his young wife, Lisa, had been called to that church, but she too squirmed under the pressure and was urging him to quit his post. Their backs appeared to be against the wall.

"They didn't hire me, and they cannot fire me without God's approval…" John told Lisa as he sought to stand his ground. He was doing his best to approach the circumstance from a God-centred standpoint.

Nevertheless, John soon heard that the decision to fire him had been made and that changes to the youth group leadership were afoot. A meeting with the senior pastor was to follow shortly.

Can we pause for a moment?

You and I have almost certainly found ourselves in circumstances where there has been uncertainty, perhaps unfairness and false accusation. I really want to encourage you that we need the wisdom of God in these situations.

Many years ago, a lovely friend of mine found a part time job at a leisure centre. She hadn't been there long when she discovered that one, and then two, of the staff such as her were Jehovah's Witnesses.

When these members of staff discovered that Sarah was a born again Christian, a net began to close in upon her. Accusations of poor quality of work were made against Sarah. Quite what they might be able to actually pin upon her was a mystery to her as no evidence could be provided. I expect you can see that this was a spiritual issue; a false, cultic spirit was acutely intimidated by the presence of the Holy Spirit that Sarah carried.

Sarah is a gentle lady who knows how to fight with spiritual armour. This is the same girl who once prayed in tongues in a school lesson while the rest of the class were being instructed on how to meditate! Go Sarah!

On one occasion a posse of the cult's leaders visited the leisure centre to check Sarah out, and even approached her, asking her not to share her faith with her colleagues!

As the discomfort and hostility grew, Sarah moved on from the post. In case it seems as if her decision to leave was a defeat, please understand this: Sarah, as we all do, needed to seek God's wisdom for her situation. We cannot assume that we know the next step without checking things out with the Holy Spirit.

One day, as many of our brothers and sisters in Christ across the globe have experienced, it could be a life and death situation for us too. Yes, it could be. We are in the School of the Holy Spirit as He conducts individual and collective tutorials with us in many of our predicaments. We often think of Him 'allowing' certain situations, but I would say He actually orchestrates a good proportion of them although He will never act contrary to His Word.

We have the ultimate Spirit in our lives so that we can deal with ultimate situations.

Sarah won a great victory as she learned a personal, powerful lesson in the realities of spiritual influence and also understood more of her own significance in the heavenly realms.

Steps in the School of the Spirit

John Bevere met his senior pastor who, gloriously, affirmed that he believed the Lord had sent John among them. Here was some clear light in the darkness. A degree of support; some vindication! But it wasn't over.

Some things take time to work through. We need to avail ourselves of Kingdom wisdom step by step. It isn't a good idea to run with abandon across a minefield, as a friend of mine once cautioned me as the Lord showed him a picture to share with me.

John continued to pray. These kinds of situations can be very unnerving and it is so tempting to want to resolve them yourself. Haven't you been there? It's not as if there is a clear next step; rather it may be a sense of restlessness and unease that tries to drive us to act, to assume or reassert some control.

Does that ring a bell: "assume control" – like we were God? Remember Satan's smooth words to Eve in Eden, enticing her with the prospect of being able to be in complete control (being "like the Most High" and having His knowledge). Acting as God for just one life – our own – would be a full time position. Surely better to relinquish control to the One who sees each and every heart on the planet whilst outworking His Kingdom agenda meticulously and perfectly.

The Wait

In 1998, Robert De Niro starred in an American thriller called 'Ronin'. During the early development of the plot, De Niro and a thrown-together bunch of mercenaries are waiting with increasing impatience for arrangements concerning their impending 'job' to be finalised.

One of his comrades in crime says to De Niro, "It would be nice to do something."

De Niro responds, "We are doing something. We're sitting here waiting."

There are times when, with no evident forward move available to us, waiting is absolutely the best option.

John only received one directive from the Lord, as he had sought His face: that he should not try to defend himself. He was under the Master Surgeon's knife, and the Master was after something key in John's heart, something to do with yielding. Speaking of Joseph, R T Kendall says:

> "The hardest lesson in the world we have to learn as Christians is how to love ... Joseph had to come to a place where he loved, where he totally forgave."

As John's situation developed, some information concerning his accuser came into his hands. He even had it in writing. Praise God! How he rejoiced and thanked His Redeemer for coming to His aid. This information related to some irregularities concerning this leader –

his informant had furnished him with the very evidence he needed to be able to discredit the accusations against him.

Oh, but wait a minute. In Jesus Christ we have been 'made alive' in Him and we now have the mind of Christ. Sometimes our internal, natural mind shouts a little louder but we can be confident that we do indeed have His mind and, in faith, we can expect to experience His mind operating through us.

That's what happened to John concerning this apparent further vindication. As he prepared to 'reveal all' to his senior pastor, he sensed a growing disquiet in the depths of his being. Something wasn't right. *He* wasn't right. And he heard the still, small voice of revelation telling him to destroy the evidence against his accuser. God showed him that it wasn't his place to bring down a man who was in spiritual authority over him. Would John accept that his vindication would come from God and not from his own actions?

John admits:

> "I realised I had wanted to avenge myself more than protect anyone in the ministry. I had reasoned myself into believing that my motives were unselfish. My information was accurate but my motives were impure."

I suppose we could say it was a Gethsemane moment for John. It was a giant leap into an as yet unknown place of standing upon God's faithfulness.

These pivotal moments arrive in our lives. They come with divine purpose. The purpose is that we yield to the work of the Holy Spirit as He develops Christ's character in our lives; in this case, the character of a sheep who stays silent before his shearers.

God wasn't yet finished with John. Isn't it interesting that we are talking about God's work in John rather than putting the spotlight on the misdemeanours of his accuser?

John even met the man outside the church on one occasion. Despite his reasoning as to who was in the right (and I am sure all of us can entirely relate to that) the Holy Spirit told John to go and apologise to him for his own judgemental attitude.

Lord, thank you that you never waste a moment! Thank you for Your patient work in my life and that, even despite

*me and my times of resisting You, you continue to form
Jesus' character in me. Amen.*

Something happened as John did that. The mood softened and the
spiritual dynamic shifted. The accusations died down. The tide had
tangibly turned. John had humbled himself and God was exalting him
and his case.

Some months later, John was out of town. While he was away,
unable to lay even as much as a finger upon his personal situation, God
moved the final chess piece into its defining position. Through another
source, the senior pastor became aware of all that John's accuser had
done, which, unfortunately for him, was serious enough to have him
removed from his post. Even more interesting is that this evidence was
to do with other areas of ministry, not John's struggles.

John was in the clear and he hadn't even been in the locality. His
moment of vindication could not have been more unforeseen or more
unlikely, naturally speaking.

*Lord, you are truly an awesome God and You are faithful
to all that is in Your Word.*

And I just love the flavour of John's response to the resolution of
this crisis. He demonstrates some of the same flavour of fruit that we
saw exhibited in Joseph's life. He spoke of his accuser:

"...I was not happy. I grieved for him and his family. I
understood his pain – I had gone through it myself at his
hands ... Several years have passed since I've seen him, but
I feel only love and a sincere desire to see him in God's will."

That's what I call an excellent piece of work, Holy Spirit.

And thank you, John, for yielding. There has been and will be
much, much fruit from your experience and testimony.

CHAPTER SIX

Our Place of Authority

"You are not what others think you are. You are what God knows you are."

Shannon L Alder

Prepare to take a self-esteem pill: if you are born again of God's Holy Spirit, *you are greater than John the Baptist.* Gulp!

Yes – you!

Now don't give me an embarrassed, apologetic frown and that kind of pseudo-humble "Oh well, maybe, yes but no, really, that couldn't possibly apply to me."

"Yes, Steve. Spot on!" would be a more appropriate response.

Have a look at these verses of truth:

Matthew 11:11
Truly I say to you, among those born of women there has not arisen anyone greater than John the Baptist! Yet the one who is least in the kingdom of heaven is greater than he.

Ephesians 2:4-7
But God, being rich in mercy, because of His great love with which He loved us, even when we were dead in our transgressions, made us alive together with Christ (by grace you have been saved), and raised us up with Him, and seated us with Him in the heavenly

places in Christ Jesus, so that in the ages to come He might show the surpassing riches of His grace in kindness toward us in Christ Jesus.

So even if you have managed with God-like universal knowledge to establish that you, personally, are officially the very least in all of His Kingdom, you are, nevertheless, greater than John the Baptist. Please note also, minion though you may have reckoned yourself to be, that Ephesians explicitly says that you have been raised to heavenly places in order that your life express "the surpassing riches of His grace".

Perhaps we should emphasise that. It provides sobering perspective concerning God's purpose for our lives. In Jesus, we have been raised up to heavenly places so that our lives will 'speak' of God's supreme grace.

As fiercely as our minds may protest concerning such an exalted position, we really do need to get a handle on the Word of God because its revelation is designed to cause us to live from these heavenly places. It is our inheritance from Jesus. Do we really want to leave that locked away in a box under the stairs? We need to 'reckon' that the Bible is true and that regardless of how I may feel about it, God's Word wins. Therefore, I will stand upon it.

When we 'reckon' in this way, we determine to accept what God says, regardless of our opinion of ourselves.

Lord, I 'reckon' on the truth of your Word. Holy Spirit, come and breathe upon your Word, affirm it within my spirit that I might live as a Kingdom citizen! Amen.

This being the case, then, when life does throw us its curveballs we need to remember that we can 'stand'. Standing is often what ushers in our 'fourth day'.

"Do you know His heart of love towards you? Do you know that it was His idea to send Jesus to be punished at the cross for you?"

Joseph Prince

You are an individual of immense worth – just look at the investment that God has already poured into you. He picked you up and picked you out. He washed you down, placed His Spirit inside of you and committed to never leave you for all eternity. Realising – or 'reckoning' on – our worth is tremendously powerful because we approach our circumstances from a heavenly perspective. We understand that God has already gone before us and that whatever we perceive to be confronting us, He has already provided what is necessary for us to come through.

This is really the key of what we have already seen with Lazarus and with Joseph. Regardless of the specific similarities or peculiarities of what we may be facing, it is clear that God is on top of it all; we are not God, but He is. He is able to accomplish what we, alone, are not. We can therefore come into His rest and stay there. God will do the necessary even despite us.

> "Man … is only a draft, a rough copy. Alone, he is incapable of attaining his full stature. It is only in Jesus Christ, the Saviour, that we can be made divine…"
>
> *Michel Quoist*

There is no selfish pride in our accepting the truth.

To exalt ourselves beyond what and who our Creator says we are, is to act proudly. The word 'beyond' suggests the crossing of boundaries. Boundaries lie in more than one direction.

To belittle ourselves is to act proudly, too. We must choose to reckon that what God says is right. In Jesus, we stand up and say that we are now sons of God, heirs of eternity and ambassadors of the everlasting Kingdom of God.

Allow the Holy Spirit, please, to imprint His affirmation of approval upon your heart. You are much loved and highly esteemed. You are going to come through challenges that face you, and move on and up in your calling in Jesus. John the Baptist was highly honoured, Jesus Himself said he was the most notable man to walk the earth and yet… we in the Kingdom of Heaven, ransomed back to the Father through the Cross, are greater than him in His estimation.

Someone who is reading this may be feeling like a failure; perhaps there is a sense of desperation and even self-hate. You have been striving and struggling for a long time. Let me extend you an invitation.

Drop it. Go on. Just drop it. Now breathe. Jesus is here.

Your identity has been forever settled in heaven. Step out of the shadows and begin to reckon upon the Word of God. The Holy Spirit is going to back you all the way. The time for self-recrimination is over.

The time for listening to accusation and its subtle reasoning is over. You are allowed to walk away from it. Come and walk with Jesus instead. Listen to the voice of Life.

Just as Lazarus was raised and began to walk, you too can get up because God and His people are ready to remove the binding grave clothes from you. Come out of the tomb; the sun is shining.

Hebrews 12:12-13
Therefore, strengthen the hands that are weak and the knees that are feeble, and make straight paths for your feet, so that the limb which is lame may not be put out of joint, but rather be healed.

The Message (MSG) put the beginning of verse 12 like this:

So don't sit around on your hands! No more dragging your feet!

Here is an A B C D for you:

A   Admit your need of Him, just as you are.
B   Be real – He sees you and His heart beats for you.
C   Come to Him in transparency.
D   Decide that He is able to perform His power and His promises in your life.

I choose to reckon on God. He is able to perform His power and His promises in my life. Amen to that.

CHAPTER SEVEN

Decree

"You will also decree a thing, and it will be established for you; And light will shine on your ways."

Job 22:28

God is in the business of bringing divine order to chaos. He has given us authority to decree such right order wherever we become aware of disorder. As we pray in His name, the Holy Spirit moves, angels are released on assignments and Kingdom reign begins to displace usurping authorities.

There are times when we can simply pray, "Lord, Your will be done in this situation." It may be that we just do not have any light on what is happening. We can pray in tongues and agree that Jesus will have His way. This is good. The Lord's Prayer endorses such an approach:

Matthew 6:10
Your kingdom come.
Your will be done,
On earth as it is in heaven.

The English Revised Version (RV) says:

We pray that your kingdom will come –

that what you want will be done here on earth, the same as in heaven.

But there are other occasions when the Holy Spirit is asking us to be more specific in our proclamation. We have faith that our words, declared in Jesus' Name, are going to set a line of spiritual dominoes tumbling.

There are times when the creative, situation-changing word is in our own mouth. We may feel wretched, battered and on the receiving end of intense pressure but in the still, quiet place of our heart the Holy Spirit may gently nudge us to show or remind us that He has placed a divine, prophetic proclamation between our lips. We are waiting for the Father to act, and during that time He speaks to us, releasing us to decree the word of change. "Go ahead and proclaim in My Name," He encourages us. We have perceived the presence of chaos and so decree right, godly order. It's a spiritual deal and it has to be dealt with spiritually.

I have learned to make this a way of life. It may concern my work situation, my family, my own thinking or perhaps an initiative that I would like to see progress. If I perceive that a spiritual block of some kind is interfering with right order, I use my Christ-bought authority to decree change. Often, I will not know what those changes may look like in practice; nevertheless, God's order has to be better than disorder. Indeed, God's order is the solution that is needed, far beyond what I may consider to be a perfect outcome.

The analogy of traffic lights works for me. I see a blocked situation and decree movement in Jesus' Name. I decree a change on the spiritual lights from red to green. It is time for Kingdom reign to take over. On the other hand, if it is clear that the enemy is causing confusion or havoc in some affairs, I decree a 'stop' to it. In Jesus' Name we change that green light to red and bring the enemy's despoiling tactics to a halt.

We can release a green light to blessing, provision, health and healing; in other words, to Kingdom values and character. Using the Scripture to do this is very effective, and especially so as the Holy Spirit breathes on a particular verse or a passage, speaking right into our situation. He gives us the confidence to participate in bringing His order. As we make these decrees, Heaven's resources act. The Holy Spirit invades a place, bringing peace to people. He draws close to someone who is unwell or in turmoil and touches their heart, mind or body. Angels are released to intervene, wielding their fiery swords to defeat trespassing, demonic activity and to hinder, bring down and dismantle strongholds.

Angels are real! Sometimes the Church seems to pay more attention to demons than to angels. Angels outnumber their foes by two to one and serve the Church as we decree Kingdom order in circumstances that fall short of divine blessing.

It is a privilege to decree blessing in the Name of Jesus. We are His. We are ambassadors of Jesus Christ and His Kingdom. Ambassadors carry the full weight of their ruler's authority. It doesn't matter how ministerial they may appear to be; the issue is that they have been invested with authority. Their words count. They carry influence. Our words, equally, carry authority as we decree divine order into situations that are before us. The basis of our appointment to the position of ambassador is not how spiritual you and I may think we are or whether we feel spiritually hot. The basis is, and always only will be, our identity in Christ Jesus, and that is a constant position. He has transferred us out of darkness and into His Kingdom; He did it all at the Cross and has identified us with His death and resurrection. We died with Him and were raised with Him!

Our enemy is very territorial. And he is legalistic. He is quick to assume authority where it is granted to him. He was utterly defeated on the Cross of Christ but until that cosmos-wide victory is appropriated in people's lives, he will try to keep footholds within those lives that do not know how to overcome him.

Some of us, even in the Body of Christ, live or have lived with invisible decrees written over our lives. Having said that, although the decree itself may be unseen, its effects are most certainly evident.

Families, and generations of families, struggle with ongoing issues and cycles of bondage, be it a particular strain of illness, addiction or disorder. These things are real; curses are real. That is not to say that witches and wizards have been mumbling evil declarations over our lives, but over the years spiritual doors have been opened to demonic activity; they may have been opened through sin, ignorance or a lack of wisdom. It may not be you or I who is responsible for opening the door but we can still be affected by the behavioural standards of our parents and grandparents.

The good news is that we can put a stop to this! We do not have to accept any family curses because in Jesus we are new creations!

> 2 Corinthians 5:17
> *Therefore if anyone is in Christ, he is a new creature; the old things passed away; behold, new things have come.*

This is the truth but we do not all live in the total benefit of it. In some families, generation after generation experiences marital strife; beautiful young people become embroiled in addictive behaviour in their late teens; perhaps the women of a family find it difficult to hold down a job.

Something hidden is going on. An evil source is plugged in and its power's source needs to be switched off.

Well, praise God, for we have the authority in the Name of Jesus to do just that!

Into Reverse

As Jesus overcame death and hell and achieved the greatest reversal in the history of the universe, so our decrees can undo the locked gates of the enemy's deceptions and strongholds.

> Isaiah 45:2
> *I will go before you and make the rough places smooth;*
> *I will shatter the doors of bronze and cut through their iron bars.*

The enemy would like to thwart us, delay us and entangle us in order to render us ineffective in the Kingdom.

Satan doesn't have any new strategies. He isn't able to create anything at all. He can only threaten, discourage, demean and distract us and he will attempt to confuse us, causing us to doubt our Saviour's promises and to shrink from exercising our authority in Him.

The Mouth

Our mouths are very important! The words that pass between our lips can be vehicles of creative or destructive power:

> Proverbs 18:21
> *Death and life are in the power of the tongue,*
> *And those who love it will eat its fruit.*

The Message (MSG) says:

Words kill, words give life;
they're either poison or fruit – you choose.

You may remember the Book of Nehemiah, when Nehemiah's heart was deeply touched by the Lord concerning the condition of the city of Jerusalem. The walls of the great city had been destroyed; God's favour was upon Nehemiah as his master, the king himself, allowed him to return there to rebuild the city walls.

Nehemiah was the king's cupbearer; we see how God had moved one of his people into a key position of influence because He had a plan!

Several times during this God-appointed project, messages come from those opposing the work. Dark spiritual authorities oppose Kingdom authorities; there are times when we have to contend for what God is doing and refuse to be intimidated. The purpose of these words was to discourage Nehemiah and the people who were working with him; the enemy wanted to stop the work. Essentially, these threatening and mocking words were being sent out in the spirit as decrees against what God was doing:

Nehemiah 2:19-20
But when Sanballat the Horonite and Tobiah the Ammonite official, and Geshem the Arab heard it, they mocked us and despised us and said, "What is this thing you are doing? Are you rebelling against the king?" So I answered them and said to them, "The God of heaven will give us success; therefore we His servants will arise and build, but you have no portion, right or memorial in Jerusalem."

These officials had authority in the geographical area and the enemy sought to use them to override God's work. This kind of discouragement acts as a usurping spiritual decree, but when God decides to do something, He effectively makes a decree and His word must come to pass, although it may be resisted for a season.

When He made the earth and all that it contains, He decreed life and purpose to it. Indeed, even before He formed all that we read about in Genesis, He began with a commanding decree:

Genesis 1:3
Then God said, "Let there be light"; and there was light.

Nehemiah makes a counter decree that is in agreement with God's mandate. Sanballat and Tobiah attempt to decree that Nehemiah and the people are criminals – rebelling against the king. Nehemiah responds by decreeing that God is the author of the work and will ensure its success. He also affirms his and his fellow workers' identity in the project ("we His servants") and their determination to see the job through ("we ... will arise and build").

As the work progresses, the enemy is monitoring its success with seething jealousy. As Sanballat continues to mock the Jews, Tobiah attempts to decree that the work is fruitless:

Nehemiah 4:3
Now Tobiah the Ammonite was near him and he said, "Even what they are building – if a fox should jump on it, he would break their stone wall down!"

Nehemiah, in Chapter 6, explains the purpose of this enemy activity:

Nehemiah 6:9
For all of them were trying to frighten us, thinking, 'They will become discouraged with the work and it will not be done.' But now, O God, strengthen my hands.

God does so, and His plan comes to fruition; the walls of Jerusalem are restored.

Death to Life

One of the most stunning examples of God's reversing of an enemy decree is found in the Book of Esther.

The king is tricked by a high-ranking nobleman into decreeing the annihilation of the Jews. By appealing to his pride, insecurity and desire for financial gain, the hate-filled Haman, an agent of Satan against the people of God, succeeds in convincing the king to issue a death warrant to the Jews. Moreover, these decrees were not to be overturned; such edicts were issued with the seal of the king's own ring. A decree was a decree!

As with Nehemiah, Esther has been placed into a position of authority by God's hand; she has access to the king and, once aware of the plot through her uncle Mordecai, she manages to expose the evil plan.

Furthermore, the very set of gallows that Haman builds for Mordecai, Esther's uncle and God's secret agent in the piece, is used to hang Haman himself.

God is able to reverse the impossible as His people respond to His leadings and make decrees and counter-decrees in His name.

Moreover, He does a thorough and complete work. In the ensuing conflict in which the Jews are permitted to defend themselves and take revenge on their enemies, all ten of Haman's sons are killed.

Our Turn

We, too, can pray and exercise the authority that is now ours in Christ Jesus. No situation is beyond His touch; no predicament is too big or too small. In fact, it can often be those circumstances that we deem to be more insignificant that the Lord would have us involve Him in purposefully.

Any situation that we perceive to be in disorder can be brought before the Lord. It may be that as we ask Him to act, He encourages us to make Kingdom decrees. We are His sons and daughters! As we align our purposes and motivations with His Word, He backs up our decrees with the seal of His signet ring.

How might this work in practice?

Perhaps someone is anxious about one of their children who appears to be taking a path that would not be in their best interests; or, more blatantly, they are getting involved with the wrong crowd and opening themselves to danger. Maybe they are just apathetic to the things of God and seem to have no hunger for the Lord.

It is time to decree in the mighty name of Jesus.

> *Lord Jesus, I thank You for my children. I bring [name] to You right now. Thank You for reminding me of Isaiah 54:13 that says that "all my children shall be taught of the Lord". I agree, Lord, and decree in the peerless Name of Jesus that [name] shall be taught of You, for nothing is impossible with You. Thank you, Lord. Amen.*

A marker has been placed in the heavenly places, aligning the one prayed for with the purposes of God. The one making the decree is seated in heavenly places with Jesus, far above all rule and authority, right? (See Ephesians 2.)

The person praying in this way has not only taken authority but has given the situation back to the Lord, releasing him or herself from the burden of it. It is now for the Lord to lead the way, and His answer may or may not require the face-to-face or verbal involvement of the one who has prayed. In giving the predicament over to the Lord, the one praying can be freer to be involved on God's terms, rather than their own, having laid down their own agenda. Their participation will now be from a place of rest and of being yielded.

We are worthy to use this authority because His blood has forever made us so. We are sons of the King, growing in our Kingdom identities. When the spiritual Sanballat or Tobiah sidles alongside you to mock you or accuse you, stand firm and declare that it is because of Jesus' blood that you are worthy to exercise this authority.

> *Lord Jesus, thank you for the power of Your Name. Thank you for raising us up with You into heavenly places. Prompt us, Lord, to exercise our blood-bought authority. We will not be timid, but will enter the throne room boldly to declare and decree Kingdom order as You reveal enemy influence in situations that concern us. We praise You, Lord Jesus! Amen.*

Perhaps you are having a hard time in the workplace. Someone in authority is treating you unfairly. You feel belittled and intimidated. So, let's decree:

> *Lord Jesus according to your word in 1 Peter 2, I bless my leader/supervisor in my workplace. Thank you for my job and for those who work with me. I decree right order in my place of work and divine order in my relationship with [name].*

> *This relationship will further the Kingdom and serve the agenda of the King in my life. In Jesus' Name. Amen.*

What might the result of praying in this manner be? Any one of many, many outcomes may ensue! The relationship in question may improve or it may not. The supervisor may be moved on, or the one praying could be moved on. The point is that we who have the right to exercise Kingdom authority are asserting it, and as we do so, we will grow in our faith, mature and bring the life and purposes of Christ into our spheres of influence.

For those of us who may be struggling with unwanted or oppressive thoughts; we can decree:

> *Lord Jesus, I praise You that I have the mind of Christ. Thank you that all my guilt and condemnation was crucified at Calvary and that now I am your dear child in whom You delight! I decree divine order to my mind and emotions; Your word says that You are the Prince of Peace and that You have given this peace to me, not as the world gives but as You give. I choose not to be troubled, Lord, for you have said in John 14, "Let not your hearts be troubled, neither let them be afraid." Thank you that I can remain in Your rest, trusting You to lead me clearly and without fear. Amen.*

I believe that as we remain open to the Holy Spirit, He will often shows us that He would have us declare a decree in a situation. Our first thought (not unwisely) is to involve Him and ask Him to act; His response may well be to have us use His authority to bring change in circumstances and to play a key part in reversing disorder into Kingdom order. Heaven backs us as we do so!

CHAPTER EIGHT

He Never Sleeps

"I had a dream about you last night ... You turned red, then green, and then blue. You told me you were trying to fit in with the M&Ms."

Amy Summers

I wonder if you have considered what it would be like to never sleep. When you finally arrive in Heaven Avenue after you leave this temporary residence called Time, you will find out. There is no wear or decay in heaven and therefore sleep will not be necessary. Sleep serves the purpose of allowing our minds, emotions and bodies to recover and repair from work and strain. There will be no negative strain in Heaven as this is clearly not a characteristic of blessing.

As far as work is concerned, it will have a very different definition to the one that many of us may be familiar with. Work is often hard now, right? It is 'labour'. But that's because we work under the curse of Eden – although, I would like to add that in Jesus there is no need for us to accept that; all curses have been cancelled at Calvary so if we can receive that reality into our spirits, we should go for it and expect our work to be rewarding and accompanied with divine favour!

Work may be hard and challenging, but as I submit myself to Jesus and believe for the Kingdom to move in my life, I can expect my work to be a blessing.

And busy as we are, we need our beauty sleep; but God never sleeps.

When I was studying at school for my A-levels, I used to enjoy working and revising for exams during the night. I somehow felt, perhaps with some justification, that I was gaining time since I would normally have been in bed. Quite how effectively I then managed to work the following day is open to question, nevertheless, there was something a little special about working in the hushed atmosphere of a house that was asleep.

Sometimes we are so self-dependent that we prolong our efforts to right the wrongs in our and others' lives deep into the night. We toss and turn, mentally mining for that breakthrough idea that somehow managed to elude us during the day. We replay confrontations over and over, perhaps altering a detail or two and then imagining an alternative outcome.

Or, we spend the time projecting forwards. What can we do tomorrow to turn the tables, to influence a particular situation in question, in order to bring about a satisfactory solution? We are looking to gain an advantage, to get a step ahead.

"If she says that, then I'll say this." We play through the scenarios, landing the winning punchline with perfect timing, eliciting a doleful apology from the one who has been harassing us. "If I see him before the meeting, I'm going to get in there first and spill the beans on Bob. Maybe that way, the Vice Principal will not need to see me as scheduled."

We spin the plates and spin they do! And how our minds run and run to keep them spinning; we jolt as a few begin to crash to the ground. If all this mental athleticism has sufficiently wearied us, we may actually drop off to sleep, only to start again at three or four in the morning, awoken by the apparent clatter of falling, shattering crockery.

So what may God be saying about these nocturnal gymnastics?

Psalm 127:1-2
Unless the Lord builds the house,
They labor in vain who build it;

> *Unless the Lord guards the city,*
> *The watchman keeps awake in vain.*
> *It is vain for you to rise up early,*
> *To retire late,*
> *To eat the bread of painful labors;*
> *For He gives to His beloved even in his sleep.*

Psalm 4:8
In peace I will both lie down and sleep, For You alone, O Lord, make me to dwell in safety.

Now, we know that Paul tells the Corinthians in both of his letters that He had suffered from sleeplessness amongst a host of other afflictions. We also know that this selfless man was burdened at times with the desires to see the churches grow and prosper in the cities to which he sent his letters. Nevertheless, God promises us that He will act as we sleep and that we can rest.

Psalm 127:2 reads as follows in the English Revised Version:

> *It is a waste of time to get up early and stay up late,*
> *trying to make a living.*
> *The Lord provides for those he loves,*
> *even while they are sleeping.*

God seems to be saying, if we read verse 2 after verse 1, that the issues here are trust and self-dependency.

When God made powerful and versatile beasts such as horses, He saw that they were good, as were all his creations. However, he also often reminded Israel that they would come unstuck if they relied upon the power of their horses in battle rather than trusting in Him to deliver them to victory.

Psalm 20:7
Some boast in chariots and some in horses,
But we will boast in the name of the Lord, our God.

God is saying that even though you believe you have covered every angle, you may not have done so; moreover, as important as planning is when strategies are conceived, we are not to trust in the planning itself. Equally, we may not be particularly well prepared or able to face a predicament in front of us, but that need not sway us from expecting a positive outcome. We can place our trust in Him, and He will bring about His outcome.

Time and time again, Israel were as sheep for the slaughter were it not for the eyes and hands of God.

"But God..." as one of my pastors simply says when considering a stiff challenge.

God demonstrated no shortage of mind-boggling interventions on behalf of his blessed yet often hapless people, and I am sure you don't need me to list each and every one here. But we could mention the Exodus and the many interventions that led to the release of Israel; the long list of military exploits in which Israel tasted victory as they paid attention to the voice of God speaking through leaders, kings and prophets. How often did the Lord say, "Go up against them and I will give them into your hands"? (1 Chronicles 14 and 2 Samuel 5 are two examples.)

Equally we see that when God told His people not to make war, their disobedience simply brought calamity. The book of Jeremiah is a case in point where we see repeated warnings from God through the prophet not to resist the Babylonians. However, the leaders simply would not yield their minds or hearts to the notion of compliance and surrender. They chose to trust in their own wisdom, that which lay in stubborn hearts, rather than yield to the word of God that would have spared them.

In the New Testament, we see, of course, miracle upon miracle surrounding and emanating from the life of Jesus, from His early escapes from Herod to the frequent threats from those who were intimidated by Him during His ministry.

Then there is the ultimate victory from the jaws of defeat. The unseeing Jewish people and disinterested Roman occupiers never saw the cosmic rout of Satan as Jesus bent His knee to the Father's will at Calvary. No conquest could have been, or will ever be, so consummate and far-reaching. The Lord of Lords and King of Kings strode forward in God's divine order and left a battered, bleeding body pinned to a piece of wood, from where He marched into the control centre of hell itself and removed the keys and authority of death.

As a Christian, you belong to that Saviour. He never sleeps. His eyes are upon you constantly. He plans His strategies for you and sends His Spirit and angelic forces before you. God is full time. Or at least He would be full time were He bound by time! There is not a situation that puzzles or confuses Him, nor an enemy that intimidates Him. So, with the greatest of respect, He can handle you and me and all that concerns us.

You can afford to sleep. He has given it to you. Take it. Enjoy your rest and your bed, knowing that the King of the universe delights to remain fully awake and alert on your behalf.

CHAPTER NINE

Time

"I am not asking you tonight, Lord, for time to do this and then that, but Your grace to do conscientiously, in the time that you give me, what you want me to do."

Michel Quoist

A man and his wife are on vacation in Tibet. While shopping in a small village, the wife asks her husband what time it is, and looking down at his wrist the man realizes he has left his watch in the motel room. After a few unsuccessful attempts to find an English-speaking local, the couple finally find an elderly man sitting quietly on the street with his donkey.

"Excuse me," the husband says, "could you tell us the time?"

"Absolutely," replies the elderly man, and with that he reaches down and grabs the donkey's testicles! "It is 3:00," the man calmly replies.

"Right... er... thank you," replies the wife in a surprised voice. And the couple continue on their way.

After doing some shopping and grabbing a bite to eat they return to the old man for a further time check.

Again the elderly man grabs the donkey by the personals and says, "It is now 4:45."

By this time the husband is completely perplexed. "Please show me how you can tell the time simply by grabbing this donkey's ... you know ... particulars!"

"Certainly," the elderly man replies motioning for the couple to come closer. "Sit here where I am," the man begins. "Now, do you see the donkey's testicles?"

"Of course," the husband replies.

"Now reach down and take them into your hand."

Uncertainly and hesitantly the husband does as he is instructed. *After all,* he thinks to himself, *this could prove to be an enlightening experience.*

"Now, slowly lift them," the man continues.

Again the husband does as he is instructed.

"Look underneath the donkey's testicles and between his two front legs."

The husband does just that.

"Now," the man says, "can you see the clock on the wall of that building over there?"

I wonder how much time we take to think about time.

Sometimes it cheers us. As we grow up in our Western culture we hit those magical ages of double figures: eighteen and twenty-one. As children – or at least this is what happened to me – each birthday brings a later bedtime. My parents gave me an extra fifteen minutes with each birthday for many years. We are growing up.

I went to my first football match (soccer, to our North Atlantic friends) when I was eleven. I remember it clearly. I seem to recall that my dad warned me that I might cry if we lost the game. I think I protested that I wouldn't. We lost the game 2-1. I cried.

I was about the same age when I first kissed a girl. Boy, that was a good day! Her name was Hazel and she was blonde and lovely.

I was fourteen when I was allowed to go to a football match with a group of friends.

I was eighteen when I left home.

I met Jesus when I was nineteen.

On the other hand, time also seems to work against us, especially as we get older. Celebrating your thirtieth birthday can be quite a shock for some; expand the 'shock remit' further for your fortieth!

I have just 'celebrated' my fiftieth birthday – the punctuation is deliberate! I have to say that it seems to me ridiculous that I am fifty. These ages are just numbers, for sure! I am glad that I don't feel the insecurities of my early twenties – life has taught me much and the Holy Spirit has un-taught me much of life's teaching – but I really should be somewhere around thirty-five! That feels about right.

I look about thirty-five. Well, perhaps forty. Look, just stop going on about it, will you!

Let me just come back into line with the peaceable Holy Spirit. In that way, I won't begrudge you younger readers your youth over mine, or harbour an unhealthy sense of superiority over older readers! I jest. Mostly.

Perspective

We need to see that God views time very differently. You will be aware, I am sure, that in humanity's early days, people regularly lived for hundreds of years. It is noteworthy that some of our Bible heroes encountered their most significant quests when they were well advanced in age. Even when they did consider their age to be a barrier to fulfilling a mandate or the realisation of a dream, God overrode such obstacles. Consider Sarah, Abraham's wife of ninety, who gave birth in her old age, and also David, the youngest among his brothers, who was commissioned by the prophet Samuel long before anyone may have considered him as one having a mighty destiny in front of him. The sheep hand did rather well, don't you think?

In today's culture of instant elevation we should also remind ourselves that Jesus led a quiet, private lifestyle until He was around thirty years old. I have never quite made my mind up about the conversation He had with His mother at the wedding in Cana. I wonder how you see it.

John 2:3-5
When the wine ran out, the mother of Jesus said to Him, "They have no wine." And Jesus said to her, "Woman, what does that have to do with us? My hour has not yet come." His mother said to the servants, "Whatever He says to you, do it."

The Message (MSG) says:

> *Jesus' mother told him, "They're just about out of wine." Jesus said, "Is that any of our business, Mother – yours or mine? This isn't my time. Don't push me." She went ahead anyway, telling the servants, "Whatever he tells you, do it."*

The passage appears to suggest that Jesus yielded to his mother's promptings reluctantly. I tend to think that Mary was discerning that the time had, in fact, come for her son to begin His ministry. Jesus was experiencing a moment of self-doubt, perhaps. It wouldn't be the last time that He felt the need to ask the question of whether He was ready to face what lay before Him.

At this juncture I want to encourage those of you who are facing a transition in your lives into new levels of authority. It may be a promotion at work; it may be a new level of visibility in your ministry; it may be a new realm of authority in intercession. It is, of course, a significant moment to step up into something new of this nature. New supervisors who have graduated from a group of colleagues suddenly encounter a change in working relationships. New authority brings new responsibilities and challenges. You are no longer quite 'one of the gang' as you used to be. You may now become responsible for enforcing some of the rules and standards that previously your colleagues, and you too, tended to flout from time to time. Some of those around you may view you a little differently from now on, but this is healthy and an unavoidable consequence of your promotion. You are now on a new assignment.

You may be married and, out of the blue, your spouse moves into a new area of spiritual reality in the Holy Spirit. Neither you nor your spouse had expected it, but its reality cannot be denied. One of you has been baptised in the Holy Spirit and is now speaking in tongues; one of you has begun to dream prophetic dreams – as real as the day to you, but perhaps your partner is wondering about the brand of coffee you drink just before you turn in for the night! Perhaps you and your husband or wife have been in a revelatory meeting and received a life-changing word from God. Things will never be the same again.

You're a bit scared but it's right.

Perhaps you've just got engaged. Maybe you're going to be parents. You're somewhat nervous, but – yes – it's right.

The Kingdom

The Kingdom of God is full of boys and girls, men and women of all ages. It is doubtless true that most leaders have lived a few years in the Kingdom and have thereby grown into those who can assume and manage responsibilities. Maturity brings us to a point where we understand only too well that being a leader is about serving. Lao Tzu said:

"A leader is best when people barely know he exists, when his work is done, his aim fulfilled, they will say: we did it ourselves."

Max DePress has said:

"The first responsibility of a leader is to define reality. The last is to say thank you. In between, the leader is a servant."

However, although many leaders grow into their calling to be effectual and dynamic, others are appointed without the benefits of experience. They have not yet made the mistakes or faced the conflicts that some of their elders have learned from.

We could discuss many well-known Bible characters. We have talked of Joseph, called to great prominence as a youngster and yet patently not of sufficiently honed character in his youth to assume the role. God saw to it through many adversities that he would indeed be a kind and gifted leader. Solomon sought God for wisdom, recognising his own lack of experience and was rewarded with it and much more besides. Perhaps he was more mature than he had realised despite his youth! Paul encouraged Timothy:

1 Timothy 4:12
Let no one look down on your youthfulness, but rather in speech, conduct, love, faith and purity, show yourself an example of those who believe.

The New Living Translation says:

Don't let anyone think less of you because you are young...

Pride, judgement and jealousy can cause believers to look down on their brothers and sisters as they assume positions of responsibility. I am reminded again of John Bevere's comment as he recognised that it is God who places us in positions of influence, not people. It may take time but He will equip those He calls. Similarly, pride can also entice us to shy away from a step up that God would have us embrace. There is nothing noble, however, about disagreeing with what God says about us; He, of course, understands our self-doubts but would encourage us to appreciate what we have learned and move into new arenas of life and ministry.

> "A leader is one who knows the way, goes the way, and shows the way."
>
> *John Maxwell*

Ever since I came to know Jesus I have wanted my destiny in Him to be fulfilled – fully fulfilled, if that isn't an oxymoron! God has spoken into my life concerning aspects of my future, which I will not share here, except to say that they are utterly impossible, were it not for the fact that God has said them and I believe that He can and will perform them! And the same goes for you! We have already seen that He is working on your behalf night and day.

I was listening to an interview one morning on London's Premier Radio. The guest was someone who led an international apostolic ministry from Stoke-on-Trent in the UK. This ministry's beginnings had been humble but it had now grown to attain a sphere of influence in many nations. The radio host asked his guest if he had any advice for those who may have received 'impossible' promises from God concerning future ministries with which the Lord planned to greatly impact the nations. I loved his response:

> "Run from it for as long as you can, because when God brings it about you will need to know it was from God so that you can stand in it."

Such wise words! Please understand, he wasn't suggesting 'doing a Jonah' or deliberately frustrating the work of the Holy Spirit in our lives but rather allowing God to thoroughly establish us in what He has for us. That can take time. The spirit of the world in which we live loves to promote and celebrate those who appear to bring an immediate impact; the culture is full to the brim of personality, glitz and talk. The truth is that these things will not sustain an end time ministry.

Lord Jesus, thank you for your wonderful work in our lives which stems from your passionate love for us. You know us, Lord. You know me. You know how to fulfil Kingdom destiny in my life. I want to say yes, Lord, but let it be You who builds it for only You can sustain it. In Jesus' Name, Amen.

"He who has never learned to obey cannot be a good commander."

Aristotle

Yes, we need to become a life walked in partnership with and in submission to the Holy Spirit. However, we need to understand that God is not limited to our expectations. How we are learning that this is true, in so many facets of our lives!

Ministries in some parts of the world are seeing tremendous moves of God resulting in large numbers of people coming to Jesus. In some cases, it is the young whom God appoints to positions of authority. We have just read Aristotle. As the young demonstrate Kingdom fruit, have no doubt that God will promote them and they will overtake many who have known the Lord for years. Heidi Baker comments:

"I find that the younger children are, the more they believe, the more they are prepared to trust God implicitly. They have not yet learned to rationalise Him ... They just believe."

I love to see children praying for adults. We can do more than appreciate the 'cuteness' of seeing our kids move in God; we can listen to them, encourage and affirm them as today's ministers. There is something very powerful about receiving ministry through a child; its purity and un-manipulated quality witnesses to its reality.

I would like to repeat that sentiment. Our teenagers and even young children are part of today's Body of Christ Ministry Team!

But, at the same time, let's not force the issue. I was once in a conference meeting where the Holy Spirit was moving in power in a time of worship. Some teens, who were somewhat tentative and were sitting mainly at the back of the room, began to be touched by the Spirit and a few of them began to move forward of their own volition into the main body of the worshipping people. One of the leaders noticed this and brought attention to it, asking the youngsters to come to the front where they were encouraged to dance and praise 'freely'. Well, excuse me – and of course I may be wrong – but I believe that they had been free before the intervention! I perceived that the anointing lifted at this point, perhaps because we had interfered with what the Holy Spirit was doing.

So, a final point on 'time'. You and I are eternal people, right? We are seated with, and belong now to, Christ. We will live forever and cannot die. We died with Christ and were raised with Him. When our time on earth ends we will seamlessly transfer to our new environment, our spirit man continuing to live there rather than here.

And there, there is no time. There are no clocks or watches. There is only day and no night. You are already seated in these heavenly places; it will help you and me to reckon this to be true because it *is* true. Young or old, whatever has happened in the past on this earth, whatever you have done or not done – you are not mastered by time. Your God masters time. The real, core you actually lives outside of it, and I pray even now that Holy Spirit will reveal this reality to you.

For this reality deflates the power of regret and releases us to embrace our 'now' with and in Jesus. It is never too late for God to move miraculously in you because the miraculous God is in you, now and for always.

> Galatians 2:20 (NLT)
> *My old self has been crucified with Christ. It is no longer I who live, but Christ lives in me. So I live in this earthly body by trusting in the Son of God, who loved me and gave himself for me.*

"Yesterday's the past, tomorrow's the future, but today is a gift. That's why it's called the present."

Bill Keane

CHAPTER TEN

What the Father is doing

"The burden that I ask you to accept is easy; the load I give you to carry is light."

Matthew 11:30 (NCV)

At this juncture I would like to mix a further ingredient into our pot, one that I alluded to earlier. Often our disappointments stem from the fact that we are not perceiving what God is doing but rather focussing on our own expected outcomes.

Prior to the renting of the veil in Jerusalem's Temple on the day of Jesus' crucifixion, Jesus' followers had not received the Holy Spirit in the way that we, who have been 'born again', have done. Only after Jesus had returned to the Father could one become born again of the Spirit.

The Holy Spirit is also called the Spirit of Wisdom, for example in Isaiah 11. It isn't an understatement to say that God has made us extraordinary in that He has filled us with His Spirit. I might add, too, that this is, at the same time, the normal way of life for the born again believer. Thus, there are times when we receive insight from Him by the Spirit into what is happening in circumstances, insights that can only have come from God. At other times, He may not see fit to enlighten us concerning what He is doing and we will need to stand firm, trusting His character.

Back in Judea it must have seemed as if the prayers of Lazarus's family had landed on deaf ears.

Disappointment

Lazarus had been dead for three days. That meant that the situation was, to all (apparent) intent and purposes, hopeless. But we have seen that with Jesus, natural 'laws' have to bow to Him.

Disappointment is an oft-expressed word. We are easily disappointed, don't you think? So what is happening when we are disappointed?

Disappointment is the delay or cancellation of an 'appointment' of some kind. An appointment, in this sense, is an expectation that we have set our hope on. If I 'disappoint' you in some way, I dis-appoint. What was going to be appointed, or expected, or happen, or be given – is un-appointed. We experience a sense of loss at not having received the benefit of what we were expecting.

I am disappointed that I failed my driving test, for example. My expectation was that I would be celebrating a pass, that I would be newly independent, perhaps looking forward to the purchase of a car. I was 'appointing' myself to enjoy all of those things and yet, with the unexpected outcome of the driving test, I have lost the promise of those benefits and the benefits themselves.

Perhaps you are disappointed with me for some reason. You had an expectation concerning me and I have not fulfilled it. The position to which you had appointed me, in your expectation, has failed to materialise. You 'appointed' me to a course of action but I decided, as I am free to do, to make alternative plans.

We have seen how Mary and Martha were disappointed. And Joseph. Disappointment is where storm clouds unexpectedly shoot across a blue, sunny sky. An alternative scenario has trespassed into our reality. The joy and celebration that we had appointed ourselves to, in expectation, have been short-circuited.

Despite now having the mind of Christ, we believers make a lot of assumptions that may not be rooted in His mind. We imagine scenarios, we chart the predicted steps, we daydream ourselves into an apparently faith-filled nirvana which we set our heart upon.

I love the fact that we were created with the ability to imagine; it can be such a potent vehicle for blessing and prophetic creativity when the Holy Spirit is permitted to rule that mental and emotional territory. Conversely, in the hands of fear and unreality our imaginations can become the seat of much unwarranted stress and anxiety.

I remember going for a job interview at a Building Society. I was well qualified for the post I had applied for – overqualified, in fact. From what I recall, the interview was straightforward enough and I had little difficulty in describing the key features of effective customer service, which would have been central to the position. I remember sitting in the car, prior to the appointment, listening to a Vineyard cassette tape. Yes folks, we had cassette tapes in those days!

As you can probably now predict, I didn't get the job. The feedback was that I was overqualified. I was disappointed. My appointment to employment at that workplace had fallen through.

On another occasion while I was employed at (but seeking to leave) an internationally well-known pizza chain – "light and fluffy on the inside, crisp and crunchy on the outside" was the mantra! – I went for an interview at an insurance company. By now I had plenty of useful supervisory experience from my role in the restaurant but, to be honest, I just wanted a local post that would not require me to work long and unsociable shifts. A night shift meant leaving the restaurant after 2am, which wasn't easy when you needed to be back in at 8.30am the same morning!

The interview at the insurance company for the advertised post of Administration Clerk lasted but a few minutes. I was overqualified again. But then a God appointment kicked in.

You see, we have our self-imagined appointments, which may or may not be on God's order sheet for us. But having stepped over the line and yielded our lives to Christ, it's His appointments that we need to embrace. They cannot but bless us, mature us and further the Kingdom both in our own lives and throughout the sphere of authority to which we have been appointed. God's purposes hold God appointments.

My interviewer, who was the Office Manager, leaned back and reached over to a filing cabinet. He pulled out a file, which detailed a further as yet unfilled post, one which was not even being advertised at the current time. This was a supervisory role in the office, one that the company had been trying to fill internally for over a year, so far unsuccessfully.

There then ensued a bizarre interview, one where we saw a complete reversal of roles. The interviewer was trying to convince me that I was suitable for the role and I was expressing my doubts! Lord, you are so gracious and so awesome!

I was all set to turn down the opportunity, when the Manager said this to me: "You know, it's not so much about knowing everything as about knowing where to look."

As soon as I heard these words, the Holy Spirit touched my spirit and I knew that the job was mine. It was His appointment for me. Please see this: that once He had spoken to me, I was unshakable in my conviction. I was later told that two other candidates had taken on this role prior to me and had resigned due to the level of intimidation from one of the team members at the office concerned. The Deputy Office Manager told me that this was going to be (his words) "a baptism of fire".

It turned out to be just that. A middle-aged lady who had so resented my predecessors, as she wanted the role for herself, held me in the same contempt and she wasn't afraid to express it. At times I felt very intimidated. I certainly developed the gift of speaking in tongues during that season!

One time at church I remember asking some folks to pray for me. Boy, I was finding it tough! I just wanted this woman to leave the office! As I was prayed for, someone spoke into the root of my situation. I paraphrase but this is basically what was shared with me: "Steve, we can pray this woman out, but if we do, you will meet that same intimidating spirit another time in a different situation. Or, we can pray that God does what He needs to do in you so that you can learn His lessons now and grow in them."

I opted for the second choice. I worked with the lady, amongst others, for just a year and a half before company rationalisation meant that the office closed permanently. During a Christmas office party, she happened to be speaking to my girlfriend of the time and described me as "a lovely young man". I like the "young". Jesus had inhabited this situation and worked Kingdom in it. It had been His appointment and caused this 'enemy' to look upon me with favour.

This book is called The Fourth Day. We are celebrating what God does as He inhabits our wounded or even dead situations. He is the Lord of Life. His arm is never too short that He cannot save. It's just that His definition of 'save' may not look like ours at times.

Adjusting the Panorama

When we look at our lives and at some of the paths we have taken, there often needs to be a realignment concerning our expectations and what God has been, and is, doing.

I thought I would be married by now. I am not. That marriage appointment has been long delayed in my life. At times I have been disappointed and some questions I have had for the Lord have remained unanswered.

Conversely, I never imagined that I might really become an author and certainly would not have been able to predict the 'how'. Prior to writing my first book in April 2013, I had no template at all for how this might come about, nor was it, to be honest, in my landscape; it was not even at the edges of it.

I remember receiving a wonderful, detailed prophetic word from Isobel Allum in Toronto in 2003 in which the Lord encouraged me to "Write! Write! Write!" I thought this just referred to journaling, something that I have always found to be useful, albeit in a relatively limited way.

Awaking at around one in the morning one night in April 2013, I knew I needed to pray and found myself crying out to the Lord. As I did so, I had my first realisation that I wanted to write a book – the desire had been there within me but I had not known it was even there.

The next day I wrote nine thousand words of 'From Legal to Regal'[2], my first book.

I was astounded when a publishing door opened, and within weeks I had not only finished the book but had also written another, 'Blood and Glory'[3], which was also accepted for publication. It was as if God was pouring out of me in print so much that He had worked in me; like some kind of heavenly catch up. 'The Pointing Finger'[4] followed,

---

[2] Creation House (2013). ISBN: 9781621366836
[3] Creation House (2014). ISBN: 9781621367253
[4] Onwards and Upwards Publishers (2015). ISBN: 978-1-910197-38-7

although I didn't put that forward for publication until later – that is a testimony in itself for another time! A little later again, 'The Unbroken Cord: God's Passion for Sexuality and Intimacy'[5] was written, which has been published. I have several literary children and all of them are black and white, with spines and different characters!

This authoring journey, albeit a recent one, has been a joy. As Jesus says, it has been a 'light' burden. And I see that the foundation of the journey actually started many, many years ago as Jesus walked me through some varied and often very tough situations.

Very often the strongest anointings in our lives emanate from those paths that we have personally trodden with Jesus. Some of those seasons in our lives can seem long, but God knows exactly what He is working in us. As we have stated, He works 'to purpose'.

I have yet to read an instance in the Bible of Jesus running or rushing anywhere. He was always exactly on time and confident as He responded to what He saw the Father outworking before Him.

I believe that God makes space for what He is doing in our lives. Sometimes we may feel that we are waiting for ages, and yet He is never even a second late.

Have you ever needed to speak to someone concerning an issue, when you just 'happened' to meet them unexpectedly? Have you ever imagined a conversation that you felt you needed to have with someone about something potentially awkward but, as you met them, you saw that the theme of your exchanges was taking an altogether different direction and that there was peace in that; it was easy; the confrontation that you had prepared yourself for was a complete irrelevance?

Have you ever tried to write a letter and re-started it or re-corrected it time and time again, never finishing it and wondering why you were hitting your head against a brick wall? It wasn't His light burden. He wasn't doing it. You had no anointing, no space for it.

I remember doing exactly that, on one occasion, when I was at university. I was trying to write a letter but just couldn't get it quite right. I must have tried six, seven or eight times. I finally scripted a version that I was satisfied with and rushed off (usually a bad indicator) to post it. Shortly after, I became dissatisfied with what I had written

---

[5] Creation House (2014). ISBN: 9781621367970

and wanted to retrieve it! It was too late. I seem to recall that I waited by the post box on the following day, hoping to catch the postman as he emptied the box. If my memory serves me correctly, a very embarrassed Steve failed to persuade him to return my letter as it had now become Her Majesty's property! Doh!

I have learned so much in recent years about enjoying the freedom of walking with His light burden. How it simplifies our lives! We can say no, if we do not sense the Father's touch in what we are doing or in what we have been asked to do. True friends who are also learning how to live in this freedom will not even ask you for a reason for your decision. We can simply let our yes be yes, and our no be no. You do not owe anyone an explanation and are not responsible should they take offence.

It is the one who takes offence who is 'taking a fence' and erecting it.

Jesus was, at times, asked why He did what He did. He didn't often answer, did He? He preferred to ask a question back to His questioners, one that probed them in inner truth and exposed insincere motives.

Thank you, Jesus, for showing us the simplicity of walking in partnership with You. I look forward to embracing Your open doors as I commit my time and my days to You. Thank you that I can expect Your peace to rest on my steps. Amen.

We are now going to take a closer look at faith, that download from God which confirms to us that He is making a way before us.

Psalm 119:105 (ERV)
Your word is like a lamp that guides my steps,
a light that shows the path I should take.

CHAPTER ELEVEN

Faith

"Faith is not the belief that God will do what you want. It is the belief that God will do what is right."

Max Lucado

Dear Bible, what do you have to say? What is this faith?

Hebrews 11:1
Now faith is the assurance of things hoped for, the conviction of things not seen.

Here it is in The Amplified Bible (AMP):

Now faith is the assurance (the confirmation, the title deed) of the things [we] hope for, being the proof of things [we] do not see and the conviction of their reality [faith perceiving as real fact what is not revealed to the senses].

And more for us – in The Expanded Bible (EXB), we read:

Faith means being sure [the assurance; or the tangible reality; or the sure foundation] of the things we hope for and knowing that something is real even if we do not see it [the conviction/assurance/evidence about things not seen].

I want to suggest that sometimes our Fourth Day experience or appointment is either delayed or simply has not yet arrived because we are not viewing circumstances through the eyes of faith.

I hurry to add that I do not mean that we should simply 'have more faith'. Oftentimes this apparent encouragement is levied at those who have already thrown every drop and even droplet of trust that they had upon Jesus. Such an exhortation only serves to make them feel more wretched, hapless and somehow spiritually deficient.

No, the issue is that we sometimes confuse a wish with faith, and also general belief with faith. Let's unpack this because it's going to help us as we go some way to alleviating anxiety and our tendency to strive during certain episodes in our lives.

Galatians 3:11
Now that no one is justified by the Law before God is evident; for, "The righteous man shall live by faith."

And we all say, "Amen." We want to live by faith. And we already have faith in much of what the Bible says about Jesus, the Kingdom of God, and our new identities in Christ. We believe it when we read that God is Almighty, all-powerful and that He is the King of the Universe. We believe that He created all things.

But we need revelation from the Holy Spirit if many of these magnificent truths are to become rock-solidly real in our lives. In other words, we need to receive 'faith' for them from the Holy Spirit. We need to receive from Him so that we begin to experience some of the life of the Word through the Scriptures.

For example, I am happy to believe that God created the heavens and the earth. But now look at these verses:

Acts 17:24-28
The God who made the world and all things in it, since He is Lord of heaven and earth, does not dwell in temples made with hands; nor is He served by human hands, as though He needed anything, since He Himself gives to all people life and breath and all things; and He made from one man every nation of mankind to live on all the face of the earth, having determined their appointed times and the boundaries of their habitation, that they would seek God, if perhaps they might grope for Him and find Him, though He is not far from each one of us; for in Him we live and move and exist...

"For in Him we live and move and have our being," as another translation[6] puts it. What does that mean? Or, more to the point, what does that mean to you? You have your being in Him. Does it simply mean that you live and breathe because He has given you physical life? Perhaps it means more than that; that you can live confidently as yourself, as who you uniquely are, because you have learned to trust Him solidly. That's wonderful. But there is yet so much more!

> **Matthew 4:4**
> *Jesus said: "It is written, 'Man shall not live on bread alone, but on every word that proceeds out of the mouth of God.'"*

The New Century Version says:

> *Jesus answered, "It is written in the Scriptures, 'A person lives not on bread alone, but by everything God says.'"*

Now, in these verses we see something much more personal and, I would suggest, powerful. God is saying that we live – we prosper, we progress – by everything God says. In this case, we have to agree that having the Holy Spirit breathe life on the Word of God and whisper words of conviction to our inner, spiritual ears is no longer an optional extra or armoury for the 'out on the edge' Christian. It's for all of us! The words of God have to become flesh to us – real, personal, timely – in other words, the fruit of an intimate relationship with Him.

This is the benchmark of a 'normal' walk with God.

> "Oh, my friends, I would fain repeat it to you a hundred times – The Spirit of God within me is a Person! I am only an earthen vessel, but in that earthen vessel I carry a treasure of unspeakable worth, even the Lord of glory."
>
> *Watchman Nee*

Now this is just one example, but as we live our lives from this place of 'close walk' with Jesus, life can become considerably simpler. Perhaps you are facing a delicate situation or a key decision, so, can I ask, what do you know that He has said to you about it?

You may have had some advice, you may have had others' opinions, their encouragements or their warnings, but whatever you have or have not had, we need to come back to the crux of the matter.

---

[6] New International Version (NIV)

What has He said to *you?* It's about your life, right? It's about your walk. We are all going to need to stand with the decisions that we make so it is crucial that the conviction undergirding our decisions is, primarily, ours.

Faith

Hebrews 11:1 (emphasis added)
Now faith is <u>the assurance</u> of things hoped for, <u>the conviction</u> of things not seen.

So to be in faith, we need to have assurance and conviction. We need to have substance. Substance is stuff – it is something tangible to you; you know that you have it whether or not I or someone else say that you do.

I knew, as I explained earlier, that God spoke to my heart concerning the post at the insurance company. I was convinced. I was assured. I could move forward on that, build and step out on that because it was something solid for me.

Psalm 37:23 (TLB)
The steps of good men are directed by the Lord. He delights in each step they take.

Had I asked you for your take on the opportunity, you may have advised me to go for the job or not to go for it. You may have told me about a friend of yours who, in a similar situation and faced with a similar choice, did or did not go for it and how they are now doing really well or, conversely, living a nightmare! This information may or may not be useful but what I really need is conviction.

I love the prophetic; I operate in it frequently. Many have prophesied over me over the years. But I have learned, at times to some cost, that it is imperative that I have my own conviction concerning the steps that I take.

The dictionary defines conviction as "bold belief", "full confidence", "a guarantee". Such confidence is not a fleeting, emotional bubble but something firm and stable – it is real, it is tangible 'stuff'.

Honestly, a crowd of eighty could have tried to warn me off taking that post in the office with 'Ms Critical' but I had a pledge from God. I had a *title deed*, as we read previously in The Amplified Bible.

A title deed is a document that you receive confirming your rights to, and ownership of, a piece of property. In our case here the property is some faith ground, right? A piece of faith land.

Upon receiving the 'faith' title deed, I don't yet have the contract. That will follow. I am not yet in the job, I have not settled into the office and met my new colleagues. But the job is mine – I have the title deed – I have the surety that the possession is mine.

Freedom from Doubt

Freedom from doubt is another reading of the word 'conviction'.

Maybe you are in a relationship which is causing you some anxiety. What is God saying to you about this? What is your own heart telling you? Perhaps you have met a wonderful man or woman; your friends are enthusiastic and are warning you not to let this particular fish off the hook; one or two cheeky mates have been teasing you about the future wedding arrangements. The bandwagon is well and truly rolling but for some reason, which you may not even be able to put into words, you are not convinced. Something just doesn't sit right with you.

One of the first lessons my current precious pastors ever taught me was this: follow your own unction. In other words, go with your own sense of anointing, your own sense of witness. Be true to yourself, for only you are you. Yes, I value and highly esteem prophetic input, but ultimately I am going to move forward in this or that development because I am convinced.

God is able to confirm to us the steps that are ours to take. And He knows how to convince you in a unique manner, one that you will be able to step out on. This is faith. It is solid, and even if it is difficult to explain to someone else, you just know that you know.

> Lord Jesus, thank you for calling us to live by faith, that substance, a tangible knowing that the Holy Spirit communicates to us. As we walk with You, Lord, we know that You have also gone before us. We invite You to lead us with Your faith that convinces us in our deep, hidden place. In Jesus' Name. Amen.

CHAPTER TWELVE

Success and Failure

"The Lord does not want His children to live in the midst of a constant interior war zone."

Joyce Meyer

The difference between success and failure can appear to be the width of a tightrope. One slip to either side and a destiny changes.

Some of you may have seen the 1998 movie, Sliding Doors. Gwyneth Paltrow plays a young woman who narrowly makes it in time to step on to a train on the London Underground. In the next scene the scenario is replayed, but this time she is hindered from running down the station steps and just fails to reach the closing doors. The film then proceeds to show us two different ways in which her life is outworked, all because she did or didn't succeed in making her connection. Without revealing the whole plot to you, in case you haven't seen the movie yet and might like to, in one of the 'timelines' Ms Paltrow's character discovers early on that her rather pathetic boyfriend is cheating on her, while in the other she doesn't find out until later. It's an interesting premise.

The world of sport also throws up example after example of 'nearlys' and 'might-have-beens'.

In 1990, television viewers saw possibly the most staggering ending to a football match in the history of European Cup competitions. In the Champions League Final, German side Bayern Munich led Manchester United by 1-0 with just two of the ninety minutes remaining. Sporting 'shock and awe' followed as the English League champions scored twice in the remaining time to win the match 2-1. You can imagine how many times those goals have been replayed on sports programmes. Footage of the event even shows a player in the German team stifling a celebration just before the first Manchester goal. Talk about the width of a tightrope!

Two minutes later, German players were literally on their knees on the football pitch. An almighty, unscheduled train called Disbelief had slammed them from the side.

In domestic competition, a similarly astounding event took place in 1989. Two teams were neck and neck at the top of the English First Division with one final game to play. And that game, by a sheer fluke of the fixture list, pitted the two clubs against each other. Their records were so similar that pundits and supporters buzzed about the possible connotations of this or that result. Ten months of competition boiled down to ninety minutes of football.

In essence, Arsenal, the visitors, needed to win at Liverpool by a margin of two goals and they would be champions. A less impressive result for the Londoners would mean that Liverpool, the home team, would win the title.

I don't support either of these clubs but the drama is still etched upon my memory these twenty-five years later. It may be commonplace today, but it was rare in those days for television to screen matches live; but such was the occasion that this match was on prime time evening TV.

Arsenal scored in the second half of the match to lead 1-0. Time ticked on. The game entered the final minute and, as things stood, Liverpool were about to be crowned champions, despite the fact that they were losing this game. If you don't know what happened, I am sure you can now guess! Arsenal scored in the ninetieth minute to win the match and the league for that season. The Liverpool management, who had been seconds away from running on to the field in unbridled celebration, now stood motionless on the sidelines.

Wikipedia's summary of the event states that the weather that famous evening was "warm". Let me assure you that it was boiling hot amongst the Arsenal supporters!

I am certain that some of you can recall other knife-edged margins of victory and defeat in other varied sporting occasions; a last minute home run, try or surge down the back straight has transformed history. Perhaps a competitor or team somehow managed to lose from an advantageous winning position or, conversely, a handsome lead was frittered away.

Sometimes that margin of victory and defeat can boil down to seconds or parts of a second. The sliding door exalts one competitor to victory and bars another to defeat. The winner walks through an open door of new opportunities, seeing new vistas perhaps unimagined. But come second and it may be that little changes at all. The wait for honours goes on.

From God's point of view, He has much to teach us concerning what we perceive to be 'success', and in my own experience I have found that I have needed to un-learn as much as I have had to learn. I have had to un-learn wrong mindsets about the Father and His character and about how He sees me. My self-image has seen some major undoing and readjustment. As much as I have learned how to discern and hear His voice, I have had to learn how to identify the subtle lies of the enemy and his devious attempts to bring me under spirits of control. We are invited to walk in the power and discernment of the Holy Spirit and yet we can slip into assumption as we observe our and others' lives, making judgements about how well we are all doing.

So have I been successful as much as I have failed in my faith walk to date? How about you? Perhaps you feel as if you have made a real mess of your life and that your hopes in certain areas lie in a proverbial casket. It's as if the corpse has been motionless for three weeks or three years, let alone three days. On the other hand, you may think that you are in a very positive place and progressing well.

I so want to encourage you and maybe ask you to look at a different scale of achievement. We all have amassed debts. They may be financial but I'm not really thinking of those at all. They may concern relationships (or a lack of them) in your life, or job opportunities, or other various doors missed or opened. Regret may be gnawing away at your joy. You may be replaying certain scenarios over and over in your imagination with a variety of real and created endings.

God loves you. He is bigger than each and every situation that you are facing and have faced. He is bigger than you and me. The fact that we are His, that we now belong to Him, makes us delightful successes in His eyes.

I am not a father. But I have had the privilege of witnessing fathers and fathering at work at close quarters over the years. Please pray for dads as the Holy Spirit lays them on your heart. And I have begun to see more of our Father's heart.

We still tend to veer towards an orphan mentality when we consider our Father in heaven's view of us.

We all make mistakes. Fathers do too. It's almost entirely a role that you have to learn 'on the job'. The same goes for mothers and mothering. As I comment here, let us remember, too, the mother nature that God powerfully expresses both through people and also through the direct, gentle work of the Holy Spirit.

If the earthly fathers and mothers that I have seen do not compromise their love and commitment for their children based upon their performance, why do we imagine that our heavenly Father scowls at us when we 'mess up' and only smiles when we get it right? I have seen dads coo over their babies and tots. I have seen them hold and kiss their young boys and girls. I have seen them share activities with their teenagers and struggle with the teenage attitudes, but it has not altered or demeaned their love. I have seen fathers marry away their sons and daughters, let them go, learn to love them differently but no less powerfully or generously.

And we, though fallen, were made in the image of God. The God who owns us delights in us because we have responded to His love and become His Kingdom children. It is because of who we are and whose we are that He fundamentally accepts us, not because of what we may do or not do or manage to achieve. Fathers love to see their kids be successful and blossom in their gifts and in their character, but when all is said and done, their kids are their kids.

When we draw close to the Father, knowing that He is already proud of us, we can come in rest and look forward to enjoying our fellowship with Him. We have no need to strive or to try to impress Him. He knows us to the core – He made us, each and every one of us.

He has chosen us to be targets for His love and blessing, and His aim is sure!

If we make a mess of things, let us run to Him. An embrace and a smile await us.

We may consider that we have contributed to, or are facing, a situation where things really have gone awry. It happens.

I am learning that it is not what I do that has the last word in a situation, but what He does. The perfect Father is at hand.

What we need to look at now, then, is this whole thing called 'redemption'.

CHAPTER THIRTEEN

Redemption

"...believe God for supernatural favour, because despite how hopeless things may look from a human perspective, God can lift up and He can bring down."

Joyce Meyer

In the last chapter we were beginning to question the more usual value system concerning success and failure. Allow me to briefly return to the sports theme.

We said that the margins between winning and losing can be very small; that last minute goal, that unexpected, long range pot on the snooker table, the horse that inexplicably stumbles just a few metres from the line and the athlete who arches himself forward at the tape to win by hundredths of a second.

When it comes to our lives we can see them very much in black and white and show ourselves a lot less grace than we might show others. Such generous objectivity can be in short supply when we are dealing with our own affairs, especially if we are of a somewhat self-critical bent.

As I look back at some of my apparent failures, I can see that, actually, they weren't. I mean, yes I failed, but in the grander scheme of things, I didn't.

Just as a parent may deny their child a certain opportunity because they know them intimately and also know what will best benefit them, our Father sometimes does likewise.

I recall this point being illustrated in a cartoon picture. A budgerigar wanted out from its cage. It couldn't see the cat that was staring at its potential prey from a hidden vantage point, but the bird's owner knew.

I would even say this: be glad that He loves you enough that He does so and does not hesitate to say no if that is in our best interests.

'No' can be our best friend.

As a single gent I cannot imagine how hard it is to bring up young children. I am very good with young kids, so I am told, but I should point out that I have the luxury of handing them back to their dear and, at times, frazzled parents.

But I wish more parents would say no to their children. Maybe, like me, you have been in a supermarket and have encountered scenes of histrionics as children have begged their parents for sweets and other items. I say, "Well done!" to those mums and dads who valiantly hold the line when they have decided that no is the answer. This smallest of words can be a mighty investment in their children's lives.

Hawkins, No!

Shortly after beginning my teaching career, five positions became available for advancement. At the time, our teaching team in this particular department was relatively small and my chances of getting one of these positions was pretty good, I would say, despite my lack of experience.

Five of the teachers in the team applied for the five jobs and I was one of those applying. Only one of the applicants was unsuccessful with their application. I wonder if you can guess, using your significant powers of discernment, which individual that was. That's right, it was yours truly.

I sought feedback concerning this travesty of justice and misplaced judgment of those who had considered me unworthy of the role. Please get this: the interviewers had been unhappy with one – just *one* – of my answers concerning the way that I had handled a work situation. They even said that my presentation concerning future vision of the department had been the best of the bunch. Just one thing had really bothered them.

I have discussed this particular 'one thing' with fellow staff members on more than one occasion since those days. The funny thing is, not a single person, including current managers, has told me that they felt I had mishandled the situation in question. Not one! It's as if, at that time, when the selection process was running, this solitary answer of mine became a huge obstacle barring my way to a promotion.

Do not feel sorry for me, please, because you haven't heard the end of the story. Sometime later a different role became available, one which I applied for, one which I was much more suited to, and one which I successfully worked in for many years. It fitted me a whole lot better.

I don't want to suggest presumptuously that my interviewers were wrong. I believe, in fact, that God inhabited that process, as I had invited him to, and He had sought fit to deny me that particular opportunity, knowing in His perfect economy of what was going to become available later. On that occasion, the cage door had remained closed.

You see, I failed to get that job, but at the same time, I didn't. I succeeded in getting something better – something better for me.

Redemption is entirely about God; it is about His character and His power, His eternity and His omniscience. It is about Him filling in the gaps of my weakness and embracing it. He kisses our weakness with His grace and makes something unique, something astonishing. The proverbial ugly duckling sees its unexpected reflection in Him and discovers that it was an entirely different creature to what it had imagined or believed.

How often has God done something in your life – or kept you from something or someone in a particular way – and your later response has had to be, "Well, what do I know? He knew best."

There are times when Jesus tangibly turns around our situations and they fall into order in a way we can only marvel at. But I would like to suggest that when this doesn't happen as we may hope it might, Jesus is no less involved, no less interested and no less miraculous. It just might be a much quieter intervention, or one of a different kind. You may think He is doing nothing and has taken His eye off the ball.

Calvary

If ever there was a time for Jesus Christ to show His power, it was at Calvary. This was the man prophet who had done miraculous works all over the region, closing the mouths of his religious opponents, healing the blind and lame and even raising the dead.

> **Mark 15:31-32**
> *In the same way the chief priests also, along with the scribes, were mocking Him among themselves and saying, "He saved others; He cannot save Himself. Let this Christ, the King of Israel, now come down from the cross, so that we may see and believe!"*

Of course, the reality was that something far beyond their understanding was taking place. How ironic – and these words hugely fail to even state the case – that the very act that the priests and His critics so mocked Him for was that which was opening up Heaven to them and indeed to the whole world. This was the catastrophic defeat that wasn't. The chief priests' apparent enemy has turned out to be the very Messiah that they could not see.

Had Jesus shown His Almighty muscle and come down from the cross as He was being goaded to do, you and I would not know Him today.

I remember watching a movie, The Net. It's still one of my favourites and features the lovely – well, she is! – Sandra Bullock and Jeremy Northam. Here comes a spoiler if you haven't seen it!

In this 1995 movie, Sandra's character, who is quite a whiz with computers, unconsciously becomes the enemy of the state as she acquires online data that she shouldn't be privy to. Basically, she's on the run through most of the movie from the state's nasty agent (Northam) and also has her identity messed with, including the creation of a fake criminal record and interference with her finances.

At the end of the chase, Sandra is at an Information Technology convention, sat at a computer, entering data. The agent catches up with her and, assuming that she is blowing his cover and exposing the state's criminality in an email, hits the 'delete' button on her PC in the belief that she has now been thwarted. To his chagrin, however, and due to her technical expertise, his actions only serve to delete her false identity and restore her to her true self. She has escaped from the net and, at the same time, exposed her pursuers through her email.

The enemy thought he had played his winning card, only to discover that the good guy won with it.

In Job we read:

Job 42:2
I know that You can do all things,
And that no purpose of Yours can be thwarted.

These verses in The Voice read as follows:

I know You can do everything;
nothing You do can be foiled or frustrated.

Lord Jesus, You redeemed us from our ultimate enemies, sin and death. We want to acknowledge and declare that nothing is too hard for You. Thank you, Lord, that with you there are no hopeless cases. Thank you that You specialize in apparent lost causes.

We decisively place ourselves and all that concerns us into Your hands and say that we love You and that we are going to trust You. We are going to grow in our challenges and experience Your redemptive saving power. In Jesus' Name. Amen.

Chapter Fourteen

The Rest of God

"So there remains a Sabbath rest for the people of God. For the one who has entered His rest has himself also rested from his works, as God did from His. Therefore let us be diligent to enter that rest, so that no one will fall..."

Hebrews 4:9-11

As a new believer, I had one or two issues concerning the Sabbath. Even now, when the word 'Sabbath' comes to mind, it has connotations of religiosity that came out of my early days of faith. This, of course, is entirely unfair to the biblical word, as we shall swiftly see.

I realise that I have been singularly unable to conceal my love for the game of football as has been evident from some of the anecdotes I have shared thus far. Sunday morning was a thrill to me as a young boy, as I would quietly tiptoe downstairs to try to beat my dad to the Sunday newspaper. Should he get there before me and take it up to bed, I would be in for a lengthy wait. This sporting treasure was packed with football results, reports and statistics. Those days weren't like today with its twenty-four hour online access to not only match results but also minute-by-minute commentary and even live footage of matches. If I had not, for some significant reason, managed to see Saturday's football results on the afternoon's sports roundup on television, Sunday morning's study of the paper would be a ride of discovery as I marvelled at the predictable and unexpected football scores of the day before.

At this young age, just before my teens, Sunday held no major significance for me. I went to church if I was told to, and for the period when I was in the church choir, it was a given that I would be there for the morning service.

Later, in my late teens, having met the Holy Spirit in Birmingham as a university student, I had some uncomfortable niggles about Sunday. I remember walking to church with friends; one lass was sure of her stance concerning buying goods on the Sabbath – she simply would not do so. I, on the other hand, wanted to buy the Sunday newspaper. Sometimes I bought it on the way to church and at other times on the way home, and sometimes I resisted the lure of the league tables altogether. As I look back on these memories now, I would say that I had no conviction from the Lord about this at all; it was probably a false sense of guilt that prevented me on the occasions when I saved my money.

I had no conviction, either, about generally abstaining from shopping on Sundays and would say now that it doesn't matter a row of beans whether we do or don't. You are entitled to disagree and some of you will.

I mean, where do you draw the line? If it is wrong to buy a newspaper on Sunday, is it wrong to buy a bottle of water? You may say that the water is more essential but that's open to debate, isn't it? If it were that important we could simply make sure that we had enough water prior to the Sabbath.

What about going out to lunch after church on Sunday? We may justify this as a time of fellowship (therefore it is 'spiritual'), but are we not encouraging some of our unsaved neighbours to forgo their availability to go to church so that they can work, preparing our much appreciated Sunday roast dinners?

What about petrol stations? Thou shalt not fill up thy chariot on the Sabbath?

Of course, we can't switch on any lights because we will be requiring some unfortunate lost soul to oversee the National Grid. I can't imagine that you or I would be so flagrantly selfish as to switch on so much as a bedside light.

Spirit Life

There are Jewish and Christian communities today who make every effort to follow a string of laws so as to not compromise their take on the Sabbath, be it recognised as Saturday or Sunday. I would not criticise them.

Jesus, of course, healed on the Sabbath and berated His accusers for their hypocrisy. It was as if He was saying, "The Sabbath? It's business as usual." What kind of business would this be? I suggest that it would be the business of living in the Spirit of God, in genuine intimacy with Him and with each other.

Not forgetting our pets, right? Jesus pointed out that even his critics would ensure that a stricken animal would be rescued if need be, on whatever day of the week it was.

The writer to the Hebrews brings us some useful context:

Hebrews 10:1
For the Law, since it has only a shadow of the good things to come and not the very form of things, can never, by the same sacrifices which they offer continually year by year, make perfect those who draw near.

Jesus has always been much more interested in the conflicts of our hearts than whether we decide to buy a Sunday paper or not.

And what is church anyway? I fully accept that the Bible exhorts us to meet together frequently. But it also says that a large number of people were being added to the church daily; most of the time, these early believers were simply getting on with life within their communities and as their neighbours observed them in the way that they lived, they wanted to 'join up'. Church was life. We are church. It is us!

The religious spirit will find fault with just about everything that we do or don't do. Don't go to a restaurant on a Sunday. Don't cook. Well, you can cook just as long as it isn't something self-gratifying, so chocolate cakes are out! So, if I go to a restaurant on a Sunday, can I prophesy over the waitress? Can I give her a word of knowledge? Can I encourage her that God has so much more for her than her shift work in the world of catering because He has seen her desire to express herself in a myriad of creative ways? Does this 'sanctify' my visit to the restaurant?

You mean, the Lord would give you a word of knowledge on the Sabbath?! Blasphemy!

Forgive me, I jest.

The Sabbath was given as a shadow of the good things to come. And here is the nub of it. Jesus satisfied the law on every count, and indeed superseded it. He made it clear that He had not come to negate it, but to fulfil it. His very person was its fulfilment and since He lives in you and me (for we died to ourselves at Calvary), then the law has been fully satisfied for each of us.

We are to live in the Spirit:

> Hebrews 4:11
> *Therefore let us be diligent to enter that rest...*

Seventh Day or Seven Days?

To live in the Spirit is to live in the divine rest of Jesus' gospel. His rest speaks. It tells us that the price has been paid, that we are now complete, that we are forever accepted and welcomed into the presence of the King, One who is also our Father. Striving is now unnecessary for we have nothing to prove. Jesus 'proved' us on the cross.

The glorious truth of the Sabbath rest is that in Christ it is not about a day; it is not about a contrived seventh day lifestyle (and I do not mean, in any way, to belittle those who seek to honour Jesus on Saturdays and Sundays); rather it is about a permanent seven-day lifestyle.

"Live in me," Jesus invites us. "Live in my peace, in trust, in rest. Invite my divine order to inhabit your every waking and sleeping hour. The Sabbath rest is a Sabbath walk, a Sabbath life. My Life."

The Sabbath rest belongs to me in a busy, noisy college. It belongs to me in the car on the road and at the pub with my friends. It is mine as I worship, as I pray and play; it is mine in the quiet and when I take a moment to breathe. The Sabbath rest oils our lives because it is Him – Him in the midst, Him in us, expressing Himself to us and through us.

He is your peace, your enduring and ever-present rest. Will you reckon it so, because it is yours to live in! It is yours when you are taking the children to school and yours should you be late for work. Oh, let Him inhabit it all! It is yours in the kitchen and as you soak in a hot bath. It is yours as you face a conflict, step up to a challenge or pray through a strategy. It is yours in the bedroom.

The Prince of Peace says:

Matthew 11:29-30
Take My yoke upon you and learn from Me, for I am gentle and humble in heart, and you will find rest for your souls. For My yoke is easy and My burden is light.

Matthew 11:30 (NLV)
For My way of carrying a load is easy and My load is not heavy.

"The Christian life is totally grace. God initiated it, God fulfils it, and God will complete it. He is the One who lives it in us..."

Dan Stone and David Gregory

CHAPTER FIFTEEN

Apostrophe

"…punctuation marks are the traffic signals of language: they tell us to slow down, notice this, take a detour, and stop."

Lynne Truss

I'm a language teacher. I teach English as a Second Language in a Further Education College in London. Although a few of my students each year hold British passports, it's probably safe to say that almost every one of them was born abroad, from a multitude of nations.

It isn't unusual for there to be as many as ten or more different nationalities in a single class of twenty students. It's a privilege to work in such an environment. As I write, this academic year I have learners from Turkey, Albania, Greece, Lithuania, Somalia, Sri Lanka, the Congo and many, many others.

Students (or 'learners' as we are now supposed to call them) take exams in Speaking, Listening, Reading and Writing skills. Some of them stay with us for two or three years and, once their abilities have been demonstrated and certificated at higher levels, they move on to study other courses or gain employment. Some become involved in engineering, hospitality, hairdressing, fashion and business studies. One of my recent learners is now based in Saudi Arabia and is an airhostess with Emirates Airlines. Well, we do try to encourage our learners that the sky is the limit.

Every learner is different, of course, but we also see common areas of language difficulty that correspond to certain nations and to the learners' 'first' languages.

When it comes to writing skills, you may be aware that the use of punctuation is not common across languages.

One little element that not only trips up our learners but also much of the native British population is the beloved apostrophe. I say 'beloved' because, in truth, people in some quarters would probably like to see it disappear altogether! I hear some amens out there; thank you!

In fact, let's change my 'probably' above to 'definitely'! Here are the opening lines from a website, appropriately named 'Kill the Apostrophe'. I joke not.

> "This website is for those who want to remove the apostrophe from the English language, on the basis that it serves only to annoy those who know how it is supposed to be used and to confuse those who dont."

Did you spot the missing apostrophe? Rascals!

You may be one of those dear people who, slightly embarrassed, know within their heart of hearts that they are not entirely sure how to use the apostrophe (or 'Post Office' as I sometimes get my low level learners to say, much to their amusement. Well, I figure that if, despite my attempts to help them remember the right pronunciation, it's just not going to stick, I may as well help them remember something close!) Or, you are perhaps one who secretly fumes every time you see the misuse of the apostrophe. You sigh deeply or frown impatiently walking past cafes that offer "sandwich's" or which invite you to look at "todays menu".

I wonder, actually, if you know the difference between these two sentences.

- The boy's father picked Maria up from the station at seven thirty.
- The boys' father picked Maria up from the station at seven thirty.

The answer is at the end of this chapter!

I saw something the other day that I would like to share with you. It does a fairly good job of summing up much of what has been shared in this book.

It's about an apostrophe, one that signals the radical change of status of a situation.

IMPOSSIBLE

I'M POSSIBLE

Some years ago, I was in a prayer meeting. At a particular juncture of the meeting, we were told that we were going to pray for a lady who was in urgent need. As I write, I cannot quite remember – I think it's always important to be transparent and especially so when testifying about healing – whether or not we prayed for the lady in question directly, or whether someone stood in for her as a proxy (in which case she would have been absent). I am inclined to think it was the former but am not sure.

As we prayed I experienced something rare (for me). My left hand was on the person, possibly her back, and it was as though electricity was coursing through my hand to her. Actually it felt like my hand was 'stuck'.

I later heard that we had prayed with such urgency because the lady had an appointment the next day at hospital, having been diagnosed with cancer. I am glad that I didn't know at the time that this is what we were praying about.

The next day she attended the appointment, and as she was checked out to assess her future course of treatment, they found that the cancer had completely disappeared.

Let's hear it for Jesus! Yea!

Sometimes we look at a circumstance and decree it to be impossible. Well, I want to say that whatever the outcome, Jesus speaks and says, "I'm possible."

I AM THE POSSIBLE IN YOUR IMPOSSIBLE.

Remember how Mary, after Lazarus's death, testified to believing that Lazarus would be resurrected "at the last day". Jesus told her, "I am the resurrection." Jesus tells us that He is the Way, the Truth and that He is Life. He can be these in abundance because He is them in His very Person. He is abundantly abundant.

John 10:10
The thief comes only to steal and kill and destroy; I came that they may have life, and have it abundantly.

In The Message (MSG) we read:

I came so they can have real and eternal life, more and better life than they ever dreamed of.

No wonder that those who met Him as He walked the earth saw a clear, discernible difference between this Life Man and those that sought to uphold the religious traditions of the day. And those who are meeting Him today are, likewise, discovering the same as they did.

I don't know if the 'Kill the Apostrophe' supporters will ever get their way. Language certainly does develop and simplifies; the desire for efficient communication promotes that evolution.

For now, I am sure the Father is pleased to remind us within the boundaries of this English language, which has swept and which continues to expand throughout the known world, that He is able to walk through the walls of the impossible, inhabit its very heart, and bring transforming life.

The answer to the earlier question is as follows:

In the first sentence, there is only one boy. In the second sentence, there are at least two boys.

Well done if you had it correct!

CHAPTER SIXTEEN

Heaven

"You've gotta dance like there's nobody watching,
Love like you'll never be hurt,
Sing like there's nobody listening,
And live like it's heaven on earth."

William W Purkey

Whatever has happened, and whatever does happen, your and my ultimate 'fourth day' is on the way.

When that day arrives:

Revelation 21:3-4
He will dwell among them, and they shall be His people, and God Himself will be among them, and He will wipe away every tear from their eyes; and there will no longer be any death; there will no longer be any mourning, or crying, or pain; the first things have passed away.

Holy Spirit, I invite You to show me the reality of Heaven. Show me the reality that my eternal life has started. Show me the reality of the truth that I am now sat in heavenly places with You. Show me that Heaven is my home. Thank you, Lord. Amen.

If you are reading this now, you have not yet passed from your life on earth to your permanent life in heaven. "Of course, silly!" may be your response but it is worth reminding ourselves that we are primarily a spirit being, temporarily clothed with an earthly body – a spirit being who already holds residence in heaven.

Ephesians 2:4-6
But God, being rich in mercy, because of His great love with which He loved us, even when we were dead in our transgressions, made us alive together with Christ (by grace you have been saved), and raised us up with Him, and seated us with Him in the heavenly places in Christ Jesus...

As you grow in your walk and relationship with Jesus, please expect this truth to become ever more real to you. I prophesy that this is going to happen in your life. Invite the Holy Spirit into your dreams too, as we have mentioned.[7] God never sleeps and He looks forward to blessing you with some Kingdom downloads as you do!

The world is changing at an astonishing pace. We can look through history, the passing of generations, and think that time moves slowly; but we only need consider all that has happened around the world even in the last few years. We have rumours of wars almost to order; we have the revealing of corruption in the higher echelons of ruler-ships as never before; natural disasters are almost so frequent that we have to be jolted into action to take them seriously or to even notice them.

And I would like to say to you, keep your eyes on the Middle East. Our newspapers will continue to feed us fears concerning this tinderbox of a region but God is working out His purposes. The way He has defended Israel from surrounding aggressors demonstrates that He alone is the Lord. But Israel will continue to lose friends in the wider international community as well as closer to her borders. And just when it seems that there is no possibility for peace in the region, someone is going to step forward and apparently work some political magic. There will be a peace agreement and the world will rejoice, hailing the Midas touch of the new accord's broker.

I am not going to explore this issue in depth here but I will say this. The world will indeed celebrate the newfound peace and shower praise upon the statesman who has brought it to bear. The Bible instructs us

---

[7] See page 26

that this 'peace' will be short-lived and will break down after just a few years. Then the true nature of this anti-saviour will be revealed.

We can only place our individual and, as the Body of Christ, corporate trust in Jesus the Lord. He reigns and regardless of appearances, the Church will continue to advance because we are part of an advancing Kingdom.

The Holy Spirit, let us remember, loves to reveal. He is on our side. It is a tremendous reality to be aware of, day by day – that you and I belong to Heaven's company and that it is inevitable that Heaven is our final destination.

I am talking about perspective here. I am not saying that our life on earth doesn't matter, nor am I saying that it is not worth investing in it. Quite the contrary. But it is as we live with a heavenly perspective that we can more effectively impact our and others' lives for the Kingdom.

We are part of an everlasting Kingdom. We are its citizens, and Jesus said that we are its ambassadors (2 Corinthians 5). This eternal Kingdom is a relentless advance in God's purposes even though we may, at times, find ourselves walking through extremely difficult circumstances. These are never conditions that Jesus has failed to notice or dismisses as unimportant. All things, we are encouraged in Romans 8, are handled by Him in such a way as to further our progress. Of course, it is a verse that you know well, but please read it aloud now.

> **Romans 8:28**
> *And we know that God causes all things to work together for good to those who love God, to those who are called according to His purpose.*

And... once more, please. Please read it again!

Here it is also in The Voice:

> *We are confident that God is able to orchestrate everything to work toward something good and beautiful when we love Him and accept His invitation to live according to His plan.*

There is much we could say about this verse. Let me share a few thoughts. I want them to touch the core of who you are because God's Word is talking about you!

Romans 8:28

Romans 8:28 begins with, " *We know...*" We talked about this in an earlier chapter. This is not the somewhat placid "we have heard" and "we technically accept" but this says "we know". Ask the Holy Spirit to reveal the truth to you – your spirit man already knows it. It's our mind and emotions that need to do some catching up. We remember apparent evidences from our past experience that suggest that God's Word is not true, and we veer towards wrong conclusions. We have seen our circumstances, for sure, but we have not often seen what God has been doing in them.

"We know that *God causes...*" I love this. Neither I nor you can make the 'working together' happen. My striving or my need to act, meddle and take control is not going to fix anything, at least not fix it well. God is the builder in our lives, not us. He forms Christ in us. Remember what Paul said to the Galatians, who, having begun on a sound, spiritual foundation of the work of Christ, subsequently thought it a good idea to try and continue the building work themselves. Paul called this behaviour a 'bewitching'. That's strong language and something we would want to keep well clear of, I am sure you would agree.

He "causes"... He acts, He moves, He thinks, He decrees and that is it, settled.

"We know that God causes *all things...*" Excuse me? All things. Everything. Nothing omitted. Our actions, others' actions, our successes and failures, our omissions and others' forgetfulness, unkindness and downright abuses are all mixed into God's pot of working.

Listen, I know about abuse. I was bullied at secondary school for the most part of my seven years there. It was relentless. I should have capitulated. Yet today In Christ I am whole – the opposite of what the enemy had planned for me. I am the head and not the tail. He has redeemed the abuse and put it to effectual Kingdom use. As I have cried out, others will cry on my shoulder. Jesus is the eternal master tactician who does not miss a single trick.

"We know that God causes all things *to work together...*" He mixes the lot in a pot of redemption and something astounding happens: heavenly activity takes place, divine creation is active as Jesus causes these various aspects of our lives to work. They work for Him.

And because they work for Him they cannot but benefit us as we are in Him.

"We know that God causes all things to work together *for those who love Him...*" If you're anything like me, you may have been the target of the enemy's accusing darts with phrases such as the one I have just emphasised – "for those who love Him". Thoughts such as:

- "Do I really love Him?"
- "Do I love Him enough?"
- "If I'm not sure about the depth or commitment of my love for Him, how can I be sure that 'all things' are going to 'work together'?"

So let's pull the plug on that one right now. These thoughts are common enough but also accusatory nonsense! If the enemy can shake our confidence and cause us to retract our boldness and dilute our pursuit of Jesus, he will try to accomplish that. He really has no new tricks, only re-runs of those he has probably tried with us many times before.

The fact is that our love for God has never been and will never be, in itself, strong or secure enough to satisfy a legalistic scrutiny. The whole point of the Cross of Jesus is that we were redeemed while we were yet sinners, while we were utterly unable to save ourselves or measure up in our own righteousness. Our walk with Jesus is not about an ongoing measuring exercise of the reaches of our love for Him, but a journey of discovering the depths and wonders of His love for us. As this adventure grows, so does our love for Jesus. It's a heart thing. It was never meant to be an equation that might satisfy a pointing finger. (I examine the theme of accusation in considerable depth in a previous publication, 'The Pointing Finger'.[8])

You and I love Him. We demonstrated that when we said yes to Jesus' lordship in our lives. He then transferred us out of the realm of darkness and into the Kingdom of Light, the Kingdom of His love. We may not feel emotional a lot of the time about our faith walk but that isn't the crux of love, is it? The crux is that we have crossed the line, that line of decision to belong to Jesus and, regardless of our feelings, He delights in us because of that.

[8] Onwards and Upwards Publishers (2015); ISBN 978-1-910197-38-7

I am grateful for supernatural experiences from the Holy Spirit, to whatever degree He blesses me with them. But I am not to measure God's delight in me by them. He delights in me because I am identified with His Son.

Let's finish our verse.

"We know that God causes all things to work together for those who love Him *who are called according to His purpose.*"

When we were thinking about dear John Bevere, we mentioned our sometimes skewed notions of 'calling'. Let's focus for a moment on the last three words: "to His purpose".

You and I are part of something intensely personal, and at the same time something cosmically vast.

2 Corinthian 5:16-19

Therefore from now on we recognise no one according to the flesh; even though we have known Christ according to the flesh, yet now we know Him in this way no longer. Therefore if anyone is in Christ, he is a new creature; the old things passed away; behold, new things have come. Now all these things are from God, who reconciled us to Himself through Christ and gave us the ministry of reconciliation, namely, that God was in Christ reconciling the world to Himself, not counting their trespasses against them, and He has committed to us the word of reconciliation.

Here's the personal part; do you see it in verse 16 above? You are no longer to be seen or considered (even by yourself) "according to the flesh". In other words, you are no longer simply flesh and blood with a dormant spirit but rather someone who has been made alive in the Holy Spirit. You are walking significance. Christ has done this in you. That would be a good way to start each day, however we may feel. "I am walking significance because Christ, the Light of the world, is in me and I am alive through Him."

"Anyone" includes you and me; we are new creatures (2 Corinthians 5). The former you no longer exists. It may be somewhat challenging, at times, to accept this as we look at ourselves in the mirror each morning and our behaviour may not appear to correlate at times. Nevertheless, it is the truth and we have to reckon it so. As we do this, the life of Christ works within us like a holy microwave, forming Jesus in our spirit man. It is only in failing to reckon it so that we empower a lie, a lie that says we have not changed, that we are as we were before. This is a lie that denies the finished work of the Cross and denies that the Blood of Jesus is working Christ in us.

> "My friend, when God looks at you today, He sees the price His beloved Son paid at the cross to ransom you from all your sins. He sees you in Christ. In His eyes, you are forgiven, righteous, precious, beautiful, valuable and close to His heart. It's time to see yourself as God sees you!"
>
> *Joseph Prince.*

Pastor Prince shares a testimony in 'Destined to Reign'[9], a book that hugely impacted me and spoke into my life, breaking down condemning lies of the enemy. He shares about a lady in his church who was struggling to quit smoking. She seemed to be on the classic addiction treadmill of 'resolve, fail, resolve, fail'.

Her pastor encouraged her to rest from striving and, rather, to acknowledge who she truly was in Christ Jesus: "I am the righteousness of God in Christ." This she did, and when she wanted to smoke she would stand in this truth. Sometimes she yielded to the addiction and sometimes she didn't, but that was not the point. God was doing an inner work, as He does; He was not counting her apparent victories and defeats, as we tend to do. She had seen herself as a struggling addict; Jesus saw her as a righteous daughter. So now she determined to stand on Jesus' opinion.

After some time, she realised that the desire to smoke had left her. The truth of who she was had overcome the lie that she needed nicotine. What a good model this is for overcoming bondage. We truly have the resurrection life of Christ within us. He is working Christ in us, causing us to be changed, measure by measure, from glory to glory (2 Corinthians 3:18).

The new has come. Hello, new person! You are playing a part in transforming humanity.

The verses from 2 Corinthians 5 above go on to say that we have been given a ministry. We often seem to question what 'my ministry' is but, actually, we have it right there. It is as we live being available to reconcile as we go, to reconcile lost people to real love as expressed

---

[9] Harrison House (2010); ISBN: 978-1606830093

from Christ's heart, that we find our varied expressions of ministry, be they preaching, teaching, counselling, healing the sick, raising the dead, feeding the poor, or listening to people.

We read that He has committed to us the 'word of reconciliation'. That word is that Jesus, rather than counting people's failures against them, was stretching out His hands to them in love. What He did literally, He was doing spiritually. We play a part in demonstrating to the world that God is alive and that He is actively reaching out to those who don't know Him and empowering those in the Body of Christ to express His love.

Let's drink in those verses once again, this time from the New Century Version:

2 Corinthians 5:16-19 (NCV)
From this time on we do not think of anyone as the world does. In the past we thought of Christ as the world thinks, but we no longer think of him in that way. If anyone belongs to Christ, there is a new creation. The old things have gone; everything is made new! All this is from God. Through Christ, God made peace between us and himself, and God gave us the work of telling everyone about the peace we can have with him.

Old things have gone and the new has come. Reckon it so. You and I have peace with God in Jesus and we can approach our Friend in every, and any, opportunity.

CHAPTER SEVENTEEN

Come Boldly

"When the king saw Queen Esther standing in the courtyard, he was pleased. He held out to her the gold scepter that was in his hand, so Esther went forward and touched the end of it."

Esther 5:2 (NCV)

The message of this book is not that God always leaves things to the last minute, nor is it that He is on a relentless quest to cause us maximum discomfort in the process of transforming us into the likeness of His Son.

We may be or may have been fathers who have misjudged, at times, the ways we have approached the raising, education and character forming of our children.

We may have had fathers like this too. Fathers can be very flawed, often because their fathers were – well – very flawed.

But He is not one of those.

Our Father is the one who, on seeing one of his sons in the distance, trudging towards the family home, defied the regularities and expectations of the time in girding up his robes and, as we say in these parts of the south of England, 'legging it' across ground to meet him. Upon reaching him – for he reached him long before the son was in the vicinity of the house – the Bible says that he "fell upon his neck". Any customary decorum common to a situation in which a son may have so embarrassed a family that he had to beg for his father's forgiveness, was thrown aside as an old rag. If the son did cry tears of repentance or relief, I doubt that his father even saw them through his own streaming eyes.

The parable that Jesus told shows us the passion of a father for closeness with his boy. A messed up boy, maybe, but his boy, nonetheless.

The message of The Fourth Day is that despite our misunderstandings of this unique Father, all He does in our lives and all He apparently delays or omits to do, is done with that fiery heart of passion for us. *He is for us.* He is our greatest supporter. He is our shield and defender. He is our deliverer. He is our teacher, confidante and closest friend if we will but get to know Him as such. This is the Father who holds nothing back. He is generous, kind, and ruthlessly determined to reveal His nature to us as His fingers intricately weave the patterns that become the paths of our lives.

This passion is seen in the eyes of Jesus Christ. John saw Him and describes Him in the Book of Revelation:

> Revelation 1:12-16 (emphasis added)
> *Then I turned to see the voice that was speaking with me. And having turned I saw seven golden lamp stands; and in the middle of the lamp stands I saw one like a son of man, clothed in a robe reaching to the feet, and girded across His chest with a golden sash. His head and His hair were white like white wool, like snow; and <u>His eyes were like a flame of fire</u>. His feet were like burnished bronze, when it has been made to glow in a furnace, and His voice was like the sound of many waters. In His right hand He held seven stars, and out of His mouth came a sharp two-edged sword; and His face was like the sun shining in its strength.*

Verses 12-14 in The Message (MSG) read as follows:

> *I saw a gold menorah*
> *with seven branches,*
> *And in the center, the Son of Man,*
> *in a robe and gold breastplate,*
> *hair a blizzard of white,*
> *Eyes pouring fire-blaze,*
> *both feet furnace-fired bronze.*

It's interesting as you gain insight from the varied, alternative readings that different versions of the Bible give you. On this occasion, however, some twenty or more translations describe Jesus' eyes with almost the same words: fire, blaze.

I vouch that there are likely to be more days ahead in which our fire-eyed Saviour bemuses our humanity as He acts on our behalf, in His matchless wisdom.

Matchless He is, but not at all unapproachable. What is the message of the Cross if not that the separating veils have been ripped away, discarded as we might passionately discard unwanted wrapping paper, to reveal the eagerly sought prize within?

Ah yes, the prize within. Remember another parable from the lips of Jesus?

> Matthew 13:45-46
> *Again, the kingdom of heaven is like a merchant seeking fine pearls, and upon finding one pearl of great value, he went and sold all that he had and bought it.*

So who is the pearl? Who could that one be, for which the merchant transacted business and sold everything?

The pearl is reading this at this very moment.

The pearl is greater than John the Baptist in the eyes of the Saviour, an investment worth the ultimate sacrifice and, that sacrificial work now complete, one who has been invited to live in and from the realms of heaven itself.

Jesus would invite us, "Come on, My house is your house. Don't be timid. Come in and look around because this is your home too!"

"Oh but I mustn't be proud... I have to be humble..." Such protests may suggest a worthy attitude but, in essence, they are misguided. To come to the Throne of Grace with boldness, confidence and an eager expectation of being welcomed and embraced – now that is real humility.

I love to play with the kids at our church. I just love these little people. They know that I love them and they enjoy being around me too. At their young ages of four, five, six and seven, they haven't learnt a lot of decorum yet. So when they approach me, they say something like this:

"Excuse me, Steve, sir, would it be alright if I engaged in some wanton frivolity with you for a few minutes?"

Yeah, right...

Actually they come up to me, perhaps poke me, perhaps call me "Mr Banana Head", or come and sit on my lap, or sit next to me or behind me, or throw an arm around me, or bring their gorgeous little faces right up close to mine, eyes to eyes.

Come boldly. Jesus said that we could learn a lot from the children, didn't He?

Jesus said that as we see Him we see the Father. Ask Jesus to reveal this Father heart to you. You just never know how He will do it but He is committed to doing so. I am on this journey myself.

Very recently I was thinking that I am not as far along the experiential path of relationship with the Father as I would like to be. Jesus said in John's gospel that He is the way, the truth and the life. But the way to where? Heaven? Yes, of course, for Jesus says that He has left the earth to prepare places for us (John 14:3). But the verse that is so often quoted speaks of a more fundamental destination:

John 14:6
Jesus said to him, "I am the way, and the truth, and the life; no one comes to the Father but through Me."

There we have it: to our Father "who art in heaven"; He is our destination. Our destination is His heart.

As we bring The Fourth Day to a close, I want to pray for you; pray with you; to Him and with Him:

Lord Jesus, thank you for walking us through this book. We just like doing things with you, Lord. Thank you for your love and power, for your passion for us. You demonstrated it on the Cross and you still do so as you touch and create within our lives.

You know the one who has been reading, Lord Jesus, and you love them. You are intimately familiar with them and all that concerns them. You know where they have rejoiced, where they have stumbled, where they have felt lost and confused. And You know exactly where they are today. And You are not late. Not by a second.

Touch them now, Jesus. As they embrace You now, hold them and may Your Spirit reassure them that their Lion of

Judah is unquestionably Lord and the Rock on which they stand. Continue, Holy Spirit, to reveal the Father's heart to them. As their love for Jesus deepens, show them the Father! Thank you, Lord Jesus. We love You because You loved us first. Amen.

"Lord, you seized me and I could not resist You. I ran for a long time but You followed me. I took by-paths but You knew them. You overtook me. I struggled. You won ... Your look of love fell on me. Marked by the fire of Your love I can no longer forget You. Now I know that You are there, close to me, and I work in peace beneath Your loving gaze ... Thank You, Lord, thank You! Why me, why did You choose me? Joy, joy, tears of joy."

Michel Quoist

POSTSCRIPT

How Much Do You Count?

"Outside the mine we are Catholics, and when we enter the mine, we worship the devil."

Grover, a Bolivian miner

On 02.10.14, the BBC ran an online magazine article about a community of miners in Bolivia's Cerro Rico. The text's opening paragraph sets the context for the points of interest that are to follow:

"The 500-year-old mines of Bolivia's Cerro Rico mountain produced the silver that once made the Spanish empire rich. Now riddled with tunnels, the mountain is a death trap for the men and boys who work there – and who pray to the devil to keep them safe."

As I read these lines I thought of you.

Make no mistake about it, these miners do actually make offerings to the devil in the mine. It may seem utterly preposterous to you and me, but in this article we see a not-so-local snapshot of society's chaos that we see all around us. Is it any less significant because it is occurring in a remote area of a South American country?

Perhaps we are simply tempted to write off these precious people as backward or ignorant. Are they even worthy of our attention? What could we possibly have in common with them? Well, maybe more than we think.

Apparently, it is a Catholic community. But on the basis that Jesus says that we shall know the health of a tree's roots by the fruit that they produce (Matthew 7), it may be fair to suggest, without being judgmental, that the Life of the living Christ is in short supply among a group of people who are superstitiously wrapped in fear to the degree that they actively give sacrificially to Satan as a kind of peace offering.

In essence, Cerro Rico is statistically proven to be a very dangerous place to work.

Fallible, confused people do some strange things when faced with unknown threats and the very real possibility of injury and death. The BBC article reveals that during the Spanish Colonial era, Rich Mountain (as Cerro Rico translates) produced in the region of two billion ounces of silver. In so doing, it is estimated that some eight million workers died in the process – a truly eye-watering number of fatalities.

It is hardly surprising that the mountain is nicknamed 'The Mountain that Eats Men'. An enormous number of people and families through generations have tasted the loss and the pain that accompany such appalling statistics.

In today's operations, some fourteen wives are widowed per month. The mountain, it appears, cannot be satiated. It provides a livelihood of sorts and yet is a monster. Fear has given it a personality. Faint hearts have turned to supernatural myth for a foothold.

People often become more aware of, and open to, the supernatural when faced with the Christ-less fragility of their humanity.

Nearly forty businesses earn from Cerro Rico's mountain trade. If I were to ask you how many of those businesses had an effigy (an actual statue) of the mountain's devil idol in their tunnels, I wonder what percentage of them you would say did have one. Go on. Take a guess.

In fact, each and every one of them does. That amounts to a hideous collection.

You and Me and Him

I am ending this book with a focus on Cerro Rico to emphasize that all around the world people are simply people. Lost sheep are lost sheep. Spiritual darkness may be strangling many but there are answers in Jesus.

Some of the lost sheep that we come into regular contact with may be a little, or a lot more, sophisticated than those struggling in the toxic gas-filled tunnels of Cerro Rico. They may be more educated and richer. In the world's eyes, they may be considered as more successful. But are they really much different? Do they need the life of Christ to shine in their dusty, choked hearts any less?

I would suggest that men and women, young teens and even children are suffocating all around us. We may not hear some of their voices but if we will tune in to the Holy Spirit, we may hear the inner cries of some of these oft abandoned, neglected, addiction-fuelled and equally superstitious people.

So what, if they step across the threshold of a church building at Christmas and at Easter? Have they met Him? Have they had an encounter with God and crossed over from death to life, from despair to hope, from an orphan, daily grind to a purposeful, optimistic sense of belonging?

We frequently celebrate the 'hope and a future' spoken of in Jeremiah 29:11. How about the miners' futures and others', too?

Those near you and around you may not appreciate the extent of it, but they have been given a gift: *you!* Shapeless lives can be impacted as they rub shoulders with those of us who have died to ourselves and are alive in Jesus. I am challenging myself as I write.

This isn't aimed at placing a burden upon you. On the contrary, neither you nor I could convert a ladybird. But we can walk with our Jesus and He will walk in and beyond us to embrace those who are in our path. Remember how those who even fell into the path of Peter's shadow were healed? (Acts 5)

Some of us have walked through 'fourth day' challenges and experiences as Christ worked His character into our DNA. We have a personal testimony now. Some of you have known what it is like to hold on to a fragile hope with your fingertips. You have known what it is like to not be able to hold on any longer and face the fall as your tired hands succumbed and let go.

And it was then, perhaps, that you discovered the true gold. You fell into the Everlasting Arms. You survived. You more than survived.

You have even prospered. You have hands on experience of the redeeming Christ.

Some of our more local 'Bolivian miners' work long hours in offices, spend hours each week in the gym or are perhaps unemployed. They take our money in their stores, clean the streets and formulate policy in local government. They teach our children, build houses and repair our computers. They are in our midst and we are among them.

They are not out of His sight, just as you and I were not before He rescued us. As we invite the presence of Jesus to inhabit and even invade our space, wherever that may be, we will find that the living God is drawing alongside some of our most desperate contacts, colleagues and friends.

> *Yes, Lord. Go ahead. Let where I am be as Heaven is, for You are in me, your ambassador. Amen.*

Appendix

The Story of Lazarus

Now a certain man was sick, Lazarus of Bethany, the village of Mary and her sister Martha. It was the Mary who anointed the Lord with ointment, and wiped His feet with her hair, whose brother Lazarus was sick. So the sisters sent word to Him, saying, "Lord, behold, he whom You love is sick." But when Jesus heard this, He said, "This sickness is not to end in death, but for the glory of God, so that the Son of God may be glorified by it." Now Jesus loved Martha and her sister and Lazarus. So when He heard that he was sick, He then stayed two days longer in the place where He was. Then after this He said to the disciples, "Let us go to Judea again." The disciples said to Him, "Rabbi, the Jews were just now seeking to stone You, and are You going there again?" Jesus answered, "Are there not twelve hours in the day? If anyone walks in the day, he does not stumble, because he sees the light of this world. But if anyone walks in the night, he stumbles, because the light is not in him." This He said, and after that He said to them, "Our friend Lazarus has fallen asleep; but I go, so that I may awaken him out of sleep." The disciples then said to Him, "Lord, if he has fallen asleep, he will recover." Now Jesus had spoken of his death, but they thought that He was speaking of literal sleep. So Jesus then said to them plainly, "Lazarus is dead, and I am glad for your sakes that I was not there, so that you may believe; but let us go to him." Therefore Thomas, who is called Didymus, said to his fellow disciples, "Let us also go, so that we may die with Him."

So when Jesus came, He found that he had already been in the tomb four days. Now Bethany was near Jerusalem, about two miles off; and many of the Jews had come to Martha and Mary, to console them concerning their brother. Martha therefore, when she heard that Jesus was coming, went to meet Him, but Mary stayed at the house. Martha then said to Jesus, "Lord, if You had been here, my brother would not have died. Even now I know that whatever You ask of God, God will give You." Jesus said to her, "Your brother will rise again." Martha said to Him, "I know that he will rise again in the resurrection on the last day." Jesus said to her, "I am the resurrection and the life; he who believes in Me will live even if he dies, and everyone who lives and believes in Me will never die. Do you believe this?" She said to Him, "Yes, Lord; I have believed that You are the Christ, the Son of God, even He who comes into the world."

When she had said this, she went away and called Mary her sister, saying secretly, "The Teacher is here and is calling for you." And when she heard it, she got up quickly and was coming to Him.

Now Jesus had not yet come into the village, but was still in the place where Martha met Him. Then the Jews who were with her in the house, and consoling her, when they saw that Mary got up quickly and went out, they followed her, supposing that she was going to the tomb to weep there. Therefore, when Mary came where Jesus was, she saw Him, and fell at His feet, saying to Him, "Lord, if You had been here, my brother would not have died." When Jesus therefore saw her weeping, and the Jews who came with her also weeping, He was deeply moved in spirit and was troubled, and said, "Where have you laid him?" They said to Him, "Lord, come and see." Jesus wept. So the Jews were saying, "See how He loved him!" But some of them said, "Could not this man, who opened the eyes of the blind man, have kept this man also from dying?"

So Jesus, again being deeply moved within, came to the tomb. Now it was a cave, and a stone was lying against it. Jesus said, "Remove the stone." Martha, the sister of the deceased, said to Him, "Lord, by this time there will be a stench, for he has been dead four days." Jesus *said to her, "Did I not say to you that if you believe, you will see the glory of God?" So they removed the stone. Then Jesus raised His eyes, and said, "Father, I thank You that You have heard Me. I knew that You always hear Me; but because of the people standing around I said it, so that they may believe that You sent Me." When He had said these things, He cried out with a loud voice, "Lazarus, come forth." The man who had died came forth, bound hand and foot with wrappings, and his face was wrapped around with a cloth. Jesus said to them, "Unbind him, and let him go."

Therefore many of the Jews who came to Mary, and saw what He had done, believed in Him. But some of them went to the Pharisees and told them the things which Jesus had done.

John 11:1-46

Bibliography

people.opposingviews.com/jewish-belief-spirit-lingers-three-days-9380.html

The Bait of Satan – John Bevere – Creation House – 1994

www.tiptopwatches.com/leisuretime/jokesontime.html – adapted

www.forbes.com/sites/kevinkruse/2012/10/16/quotes-on-leadership/

www.brainyquote.com/quotes/topics/topic_time.html#0ImOzJToVRHAYpM6.99

The Red Sea Rules – Robert J Morgan – 2001 – Thomas Nelson Publishers

www.goodreads.com/quotes/tag/self-esteem?page=3

www.goodreads.com/quotes/tag/bitterness

www.goodreads.com/quotes/tag/sleep?page=5

www.goodreads.com/quotes/tag/punctuation?page=2

If Not for the Grace of God – Joyce Meyer – 1995 – Warner Faith

www.biblegateway.com/resources/commentaries/IVP-NT/John/Jesus-Raises-Lazarus

www.goodreads.com/quotes/tag/hope

Discipline: The Glad Surrender – Elizabeth Elliot – 1982 – OM Publishing

Prayers of Life – Michel Quoist – 1963 – Gill and Macmillan

When Heaven is Silent – Ron Dunn – 1994 – Authentic Media

God Meant It for Good – R T Kendall – 1988 – Morning Star Publications

100 Days of Favor – Joseph Prince – 2011 – Charisma House

en.wikipedia.org/wiki/Crucible

Experiencing the Depths of Jesus Christ – Jeanne Guyon – 2005 – Seedsowers Publishing.

The Power of Right Believing – Joseph Prince – 2013 – Faithwords

Meet Christ and Live! – Michel Quoist – 1973 – Gill and Macmillan

www.goodreads.com/quotes/tag/faith

www.goodreads.com/quotes/tag/heaven

www.searchquotes.com/search/I_Want_To_Know/4/

www.imdb.com/character/ch0030013/quotes

The Rest of the Gospel – Dan Stone and David Gregory – 2000 – One Press

Reckless Devotion – Rolland and Heidi Baker – 2014 – River Publishing and Media Ltd

www.bbc.co.uk/news/magazine-29448079 BBC Article: accessed 02/10/14 Cerro Rico: Devil worship on the man-eating mountain – by Catharina Moh BBC News, Bolivia

The Normal Christian Life – Watchman Nee – p 141 – accessed 04/10/14 at www.holdingtotruth.com/2013/02/18/15-favorite-quotes-from-the-normal-christian-life-by-watchman-nee/

en.wikipedia.org/wiki/Liverpool_F.C._0%E2%80%932_Arsenal_F.C._%2826_May_1989%29 – accessed 04/10/14

Also by the Author

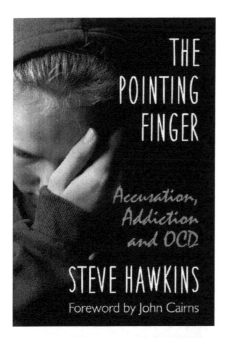

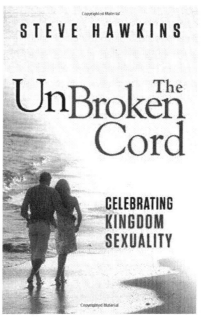

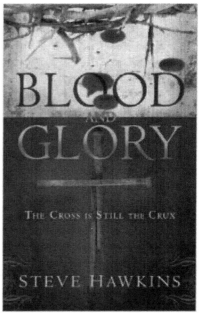